BOOKSTORE ROMANCE

Love Speaks Volumes

JUDITH ROSEN

BRANDEIS UNIVERSITY PRESS
WALTHAM, MASSACHUSETTS

for Chuck and Liz

Brandeis University Press

Manufactured in the Czech Republic
Designed and composed in Informative, Vogue Sans, and Lathi by Endpaper Studio, endpaperstudio.com
Cover photograph by Warren Lane, hello@warrenlanephotography.com

Library of Congress Cataloging-in-Publication Data
Names: Rosen, Judith (Editor), author.
Title: Bookstore romance : love speaks volumes / Judith Rosen.
Description: Waltham, Massachusetts : Brandeis University Press, 2025. | Summary: “A celebration of love and of bricks-and-mortar bookstores told through the stories—in words and pictures—of couples who chose to get engaged, and sometimes married, in bookstores”—Provided by publisher.
Identifiers: LCCN 2024031869 | ISBN 9781684582549 (cloth)
Subjects: LCSH: Couples—Anecdotes. | Bookstores—Anecdotes. | Couples—Pictorial works. | Bookstores—Pictorial works.
Classification: LCC HQ801 .R693 2025 | DDC 306.84/1—dc23/eng/20240812
LC record available at https://lccn.loc.gov/2024031869

5 4 3 2 1

Photography credits by page number: **vii:** Courtesy of Jeffrey Mayersohn. **3:** © Israel Carbajal, Luxnoire Films. **4–5:** © Adore Photography, LLC. **6–7:** © Amanda Macchia. **8–10:** © A Tale Ahead. **11–13:** Courtesy of Trident Booksellers & Café. **14–15:** © Charlie Schumann, courtesy of City Lit Books. **17–18:** © Dafydd Wood, courtesy of Northshire Bookstore. **20–21:** © Jess Capozzola, Focus on Joy Photography. **22–23:** © Carissa Woo Photography. **24–25:** © Kelly Spaine Photography. **26, 28–29:** © Megan Kantor. **30, 33:** Courtesy of Danny and Lucy. **31:** © Leah Koch. **34–36:** © TMT Weddings, Mark Torres. **37–39:** Courtesy of Emily and Samuel. **40–41:** © Bob Daemmrich. **42–44:** © Ashley Wall. **48-49:** © Emily Ross, Dreamy Elk Photography & Design, LLC. **50-52:** © Stephanie Berenson. **53–55:** © Erica Camille. **56–59:** © Aspen Cavalcanti. **60–62:** © Al Fann Photography. **65:** © Michelle Johnsen. **66–69:** © Warren Lane. **70–71:** © Ashley Benham. **72–73:** © Stella Dolce Photography. **74–75:** © Linda Shevel. **77:** © Sarah Hollenbeck, courtesy of Women & Children First.

There are as many forms of love as there are moments in time.

—Jane Austen

Contents

Foreword by Jeffrey Mayersohn **vi**

Introduction **viii**

PROPOSALS AND ENGAGEMENTS

Michael and Paige | Bart's Books (Ojai, California) **2**

Stephanie and Thomas | Boulder Book Store (Boulder, Colorado) **4**

Breanne and Natalie | Brookline Booksmith (Brookline, Massachusetts) **6**

Jennifer and Warren | City Lights Bookstore (San Francisco, California) **8**

FRIDAY I'M IN LOVE: DATE NIGHT AT THE BOOKSTORE 11

Alexa and David | City Lit Books (Chicago, Illinois) **14**

Kelly and Steven | Northshire Bookstore (Manchester Center, Vermont) **17**

Clare and Stephen | Kramers (Washington, DC) **20**

Dru and Kristen | The Last Bookstore (Los Angeles, California) **23**

Brendan and Sam | Old Town Books (Alexandria, Virginia) **24**

WHERE ROMANCE COMES FIRST: THE RIPPED BODICE 27

Danny and Lucy | The Ripped Bodice (Culver City, California) **31**

Caroline and Michael | RJ Julia Booksellers (Madison, Connecticut) **34**

Emily and Samuel | Shakespeare and Company (Paris, France) **37**

Nikki and Ryan | Texas Book Festival (Austin, Texas) **40**

Daman and Jena | Vroman's Bookstore (Pasadena, California) **43**

WEDDINGS AND RECEPTIONS

Breonna | Brazos Bookstore (Houston, Texas) **48**

Caitrin and Keith | Beacon Hill Books & Cafe (Boston, Massachusetts) **50**

Anna and Jill | Housing Works Bookstore (New York, New York) **53**

Ryan and Sarah | Island Books (Mercer Island, Washington) **56**

Erin and Kim | King's Books (Tacoma, Washington) **61**

MATRIMONY MONDAYS 64

Kaylah and Nick | More Than Words (Boston, Massachusetts) **67**

Arthur and Audrey | Novel Bookstore (Memphis, Tennessee) **70**

Andrew and Niki | Parnassus Books (Nashville, Tennessee) **73**

Kate and Michael | Penguin Bookshop (Sewickley, Pennsylvania) **75**

Abigail and Jason | Women & Children First (Chicago, Illinois) **76**

Afterword **78**

Acknowledgments **79**

Foreword

BOOKSTORE ROMANCE and the romance of bookstores have both been persistent themes throughout my relationship with my wife, beginning long before we bought Harvard Book Store. On Linda's very first day at the high-tech company where I worked, she and I rode up in the elevator together. Although she paid me no notice, by the time I got off at my floor, I was in love. My shyness being a significant obstacle, it wasn't until five months later, in February 1981, that we had dinner and planned our first day together. We agreed to meet at the now closed WordsWorth Books in Harvard Square, Cambridge, Massachusetts.

This was, perhaps, a strange decision, since the forecast predicted magnificent weather. We might have chosen some historic site in Harvard Yard as a rendezvous point instead. To add to the mystery, neither of us knew that the other loved books. But, somehow, it was preordained that we should spend some of our first moments together wandering the stacks of a bookstore.

This set a pattern that has persisted throughout our life. In a very real sense, we've striven to recreate that first day at every opportunity. As our children were growing up, our favorite family pastime was to visit Harvard Square on Saturday night, both to see the street performers but, more importantly, to browse and shop at Harvard Book Store, which quickly became our favorite bookstore.

Vacations involved trips to bookstores, most notably in the UK and Ireland. Thus, we've spent hours at wonderful institutions like Palas Print within Caernarfon's town walls, Blackwell's and Foyles, and the multitude of bookshops in Dublin and Edinburgh. The high point of our biblio-tourism was a pilgrimage to Hay-on-Wye, an entire town built around bookstores and therefore a holy site for bibliophiles.

Since a guiding principle of ours is that every visit to an independent bookstore requires a purchase, perhaps one downside to our lifelong obsession is that, at last count, our home contains more than 12,000 volumes. Even more significantly, for our retirement project, the universe moved us to seek to buy a bookstore. Incredibly, almost at the very moment we started looking, Frank Kramer put Harvard Book Store, where we had spent so many happy times, up for sale. For us, the allure continues as we age.

I've contemplated this seemingly magical allure often. Having spent countless hours in what became our store, I've no-

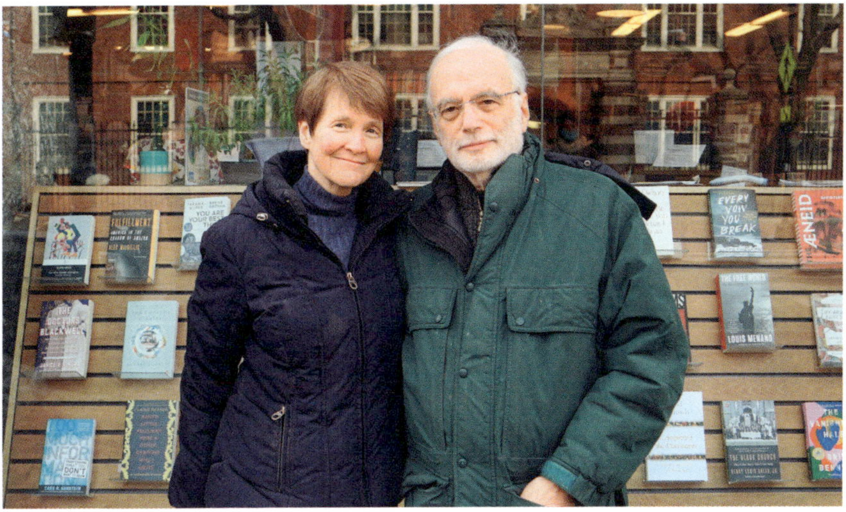

Linda and Jeffrey in front of the bookstore that they co-own.

ticed that many customers enter and observe the floor-to-ceiling walls of books with a look of genuine joy—something that likely doesn't occur when they enter any other retail establishment. Why do bookstores elicit this kind of reaction? What is it about them that drives some people to celebrate life's key events among their stacks? I don't really know, even though I am afflicted more than most. I've contemplated multiple theories but have resolved to be content with the idea that the desire to tell and hear stories runs deep within humankind, so profoundly that it defies a coherent explanation. And stories, both fiction and nonfiction, are what bookstores offer.

As a co-owner, it is perhaps self-serving to say this, but I think more than any other institution, bookstores have a valid claim to be the quintessential "third place," that which we look to inhabit apart from home and work. This has certainly been the case for our family . . . and clearly for the people whose stories grace the pages of this book.

—Jeffrey Mayersohn, co-owner, Harvard Book Store, Cambridge, Massachusetts

Introduction

THOUGH VIRGIL WROTE "love conquers all" (*omni vincit amor*) more than two thousand years ago, this is just as true today. That is why it's been such a pleasure for me to put together these tales of love, all set in every romantic book lover's favorite place, a bookstore. It's why some of the beautiful photographs included show a giddy happiness, whether a couple is getting engaged or getting married.

In some images, the happiness is also leavened with surprise. Jena turned around at Vroman's Bookstore in Pasadena, California, to find her boyfriend, who she thought was far away and unable to come to a big event that evening, drop to one knee to propose.

Alexa knew that David was planning to ask her to marry him after she accidentally saw his emails to City Lit Books in Chicago. Afterwards he told her that since she had ruined his plans, it would happen much later. But when he proposed on the originally planned date, she was still surprised and very happy. Look closely at the photo, and you can also see the couple's joy reflected on the faces of those who were in the bookstore at the same time.

When Steven asked Kelly to marry him, he couldn't have been happier. But neither could the booksellers in the store. He overheard one whisper, "I came back early from my break just to see this!"

Stephen tried to plan every detail of his proposal to Clare at Kramer Books (now Kramers) in Washington, DC, down to proposing in the window so that they would be framed under the sign in their engagement photos. Little did he know that the lit window would draw fans of real-life romance like moths to a candle and that an audience would gather outside the bookstore waiting for the couple to arrive.

At the height of the Covid pandemic, a number of couples had to change their plans, but the ones I spoke with had no regrets. Some even found a greater sense of happiness than they might have had with Plan A. That was the case for Ryan and Sarah, who had two weeks to cancel their destination wedding and move it closer to home. Fortunately, a local bookseller offered her store, Island Books on Mercer Island, Washington, for the wedding ceremony. Later Sarah said that she got the wedding that she didn't know she wanted.

Abigail and Jason had wanted a destination wedding. Instead, they married in Chicago at their favorite bookstore, Women & Children First, where they had spent much of their dating life. Their wedding was broadcast via Zoom. Like everyone in the store, they were were masked. Still, the couple had no regrets and even bought a book on their way out.

For booksellers, too, there is nothing quite like a wedding or a proposal. "It was the most exciting day of my life when someone asked if they could propose at the store," said Leah Koch, co-owner of The Ripped Bodice bookstores in Culver City, California, and Brooklyn, New York. She was excited to hold weddings at both stores for the first time last year.

Wherever the bookish venue, engagements and weddings continue to bring smiles to the faces of all who behold the happy couple. May the photos and stories collected in this book bring a similar feeling of joy, and perhaps love, to every reader.

—Judith Rosen

PROPOSALS *and* ENGAGEMENTS

MICHAEL AND PAIGE

Engaged: December 2, 2022 | Bart's Books (Ojai, California)

TAKE IT OUTSIDE: In many relationships, there is one person who is a mega-reader. That's the case with Michael and Paige, who met in 2018. "Paige has always loved to read and has her own library at our home," he said. Under her influence he reads more than ever, especially graphic novels, and listens to audiobooks.

When it came time to propose, Michael knew it had to be at eighty-year-old Bart's Books, which Paige had always wanted to visit. Not only is it the world's largest outdoor bookstore, but it frequently appears on Top 10 lists of the world's most beautiful bookshops.

Michael suggested an overnight trip from their home in Orange County to Ojai Valley to take photos for their Christmas cards at an olive oil farm. But when they got there, he told Paige that he was lost and couldn't find the grove. Instead, he brought her to Bart's Books, which he had secretly rented for an hour before the store opened for the day. They had the place to themselves as they wandered among the shelves of books covered by tin roofing and surrounded by greenery. Michael found a promising spot between Psychology and Self-Help/Inspiration. There he dropped to one knee and asked Paige to marry him.

A professional photographer was at the ready and took lots of photos, just as Michael had promised. But these weren't for Christmas cards. Instead, Michael and Paige framed them and displayed them at their wedding during cocktail hour and in the reception hall.

Since getting married, Paige's interest in books has only grown. Recently she started studying to get her library science degree. As she told the *Los Angeles Times*, for a story on the iconic bookstore, "My whole life revolves around reading and books. I couldn't have asked for anything better [than getting engaged at Bart's]."

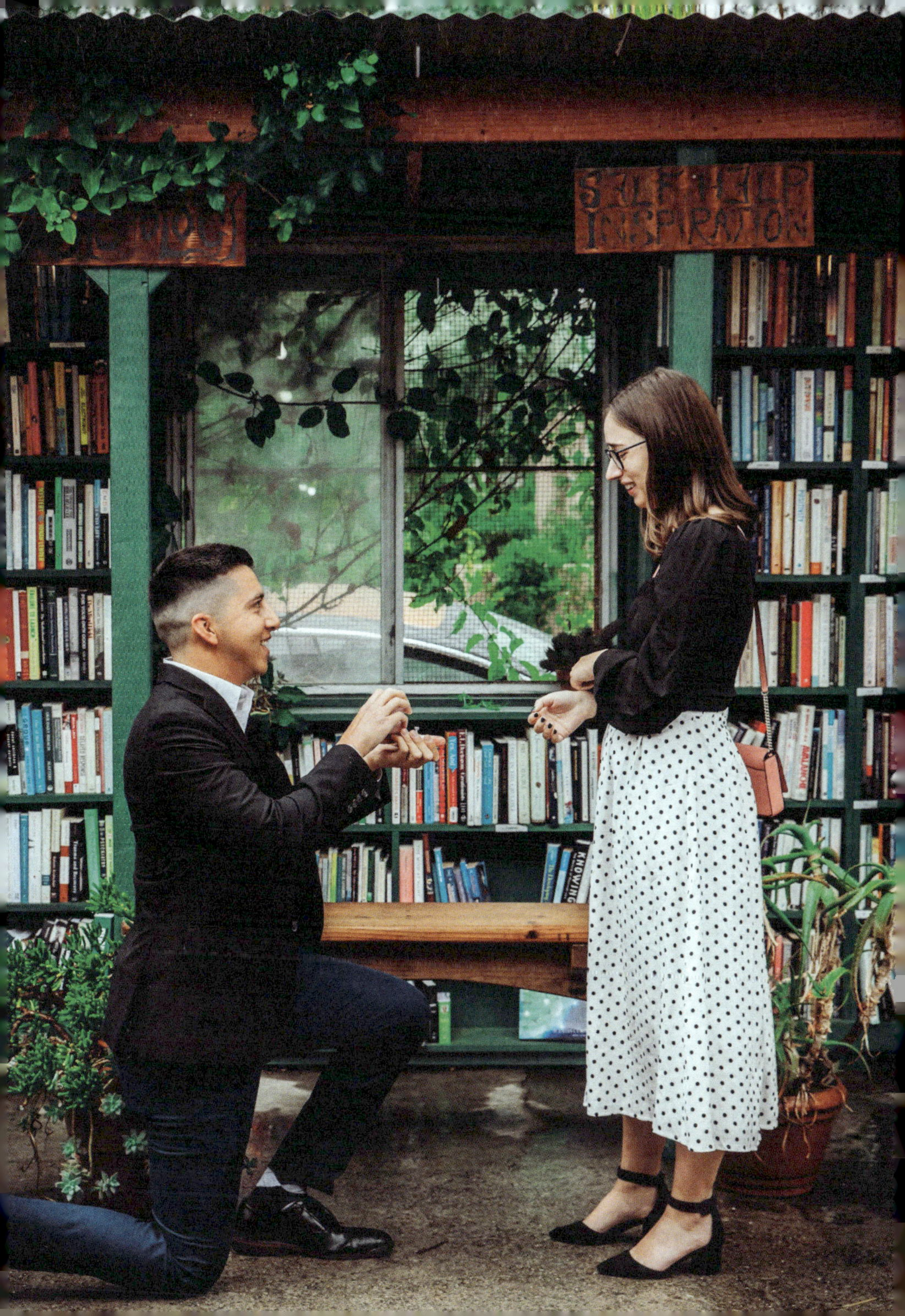
SELF HELP
INSPIRATION

STEPHANIE AND THOMAS

Engaged: March 14, 2014 | Boulder Book Store (Boulder, Colorado)

THE SKY'S THE LIMIT: When Stephanie first moved to Boulder, she went to a Halloween party with her sister and met Gandalf, aka Thomas, which wasn't necessarily love at first sight. But the two did have a lot in common. They are both fantasy fans and especially like the works of J. R. R. Tolkien and Terry Pratchett. Plus, Thomas was in her sister's astrophysics program.

As a longtime bookseller, Stephanie was particularly impressed with Thomas's knowledge of the cosmos and literature. A scientist, he had minored in Norse literature as an undergraduate, while Stephanie learned about books firsthand, starting as an intern at Malaprop's Bookstore/Cafe in Asheville when she was a junior in college.

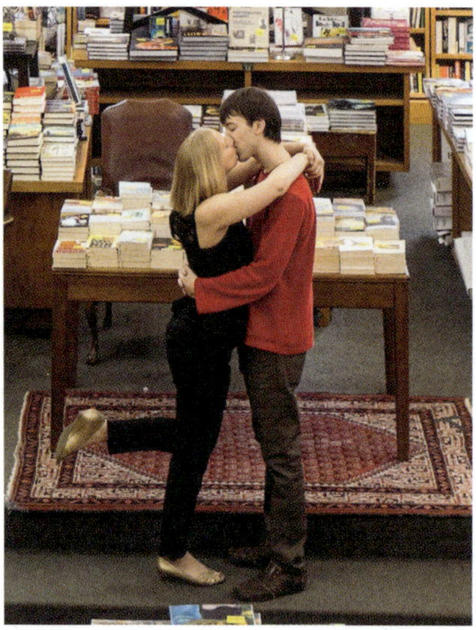

Soon after coming to Colorado, Stephanie continued her bookish education at Boulder Book Store, where she has now worked for close to twenty years. After a variety of jobs there, she currently manages the store's marketing and promotions.

After Stephanie and Thomas took their relationship to the next level and got engaged, they wanted to celebrate with photographs at two places special to them, Boulder Books and Colorado University Observatory. At the bookstore, the couple took advantage of the dramatic ballroom and picked out books to hold by some of their favorite authors—Mary Roach, Carl Sagan, and Tolkien— in photos for their save-the-date announcements.

Although the wedding took place at the Denver Museum of Nature and Science, Stephanie and Thomas didn't neglect their literary leanings. They exchanged vows under a book arch, and Stephanie created bookish décor to make their wedding memorable. While Thomas was finishing his PhD in Iowa, she spent many evenings and weekends repurposing books that were too damaged to resell in the store's used book department. She turned some into vases by removing the spines, then filled them with flowers made from book pages.

While Thomas's career may be linked to the stars, the pair continue to make books a big part of their lives. They read aloud to each other. "It can be nice to watch TV," Stephanie said. "But it's nice to be a little more cerebral."

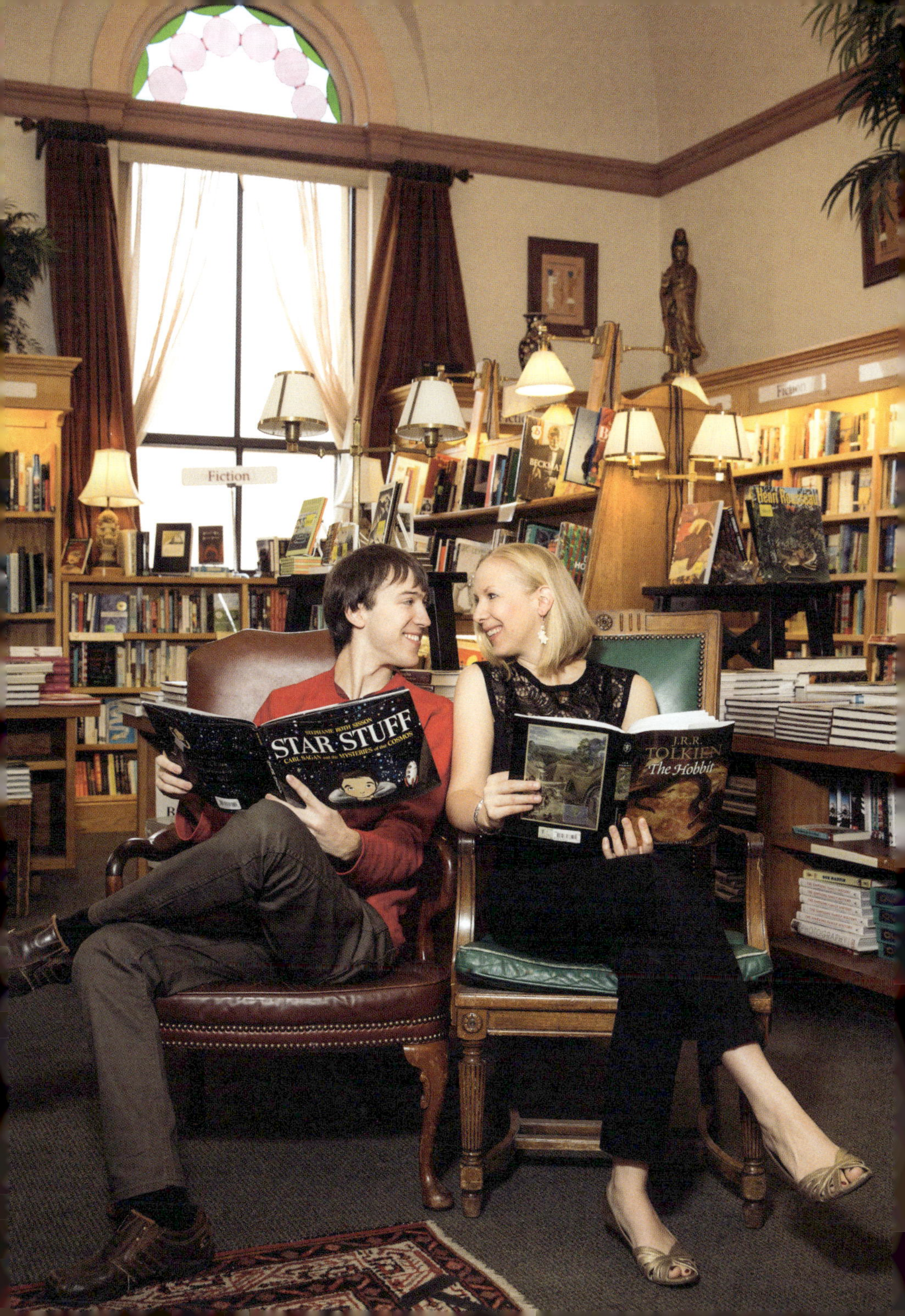
Fiction
STEPHANIE ROTH SISSON
STAR STUFF
CARL SAGAN and the MYSTERIES of the COSMOS
J.R.R. TOLKIEN
The Hobbit
Henri Rousseau

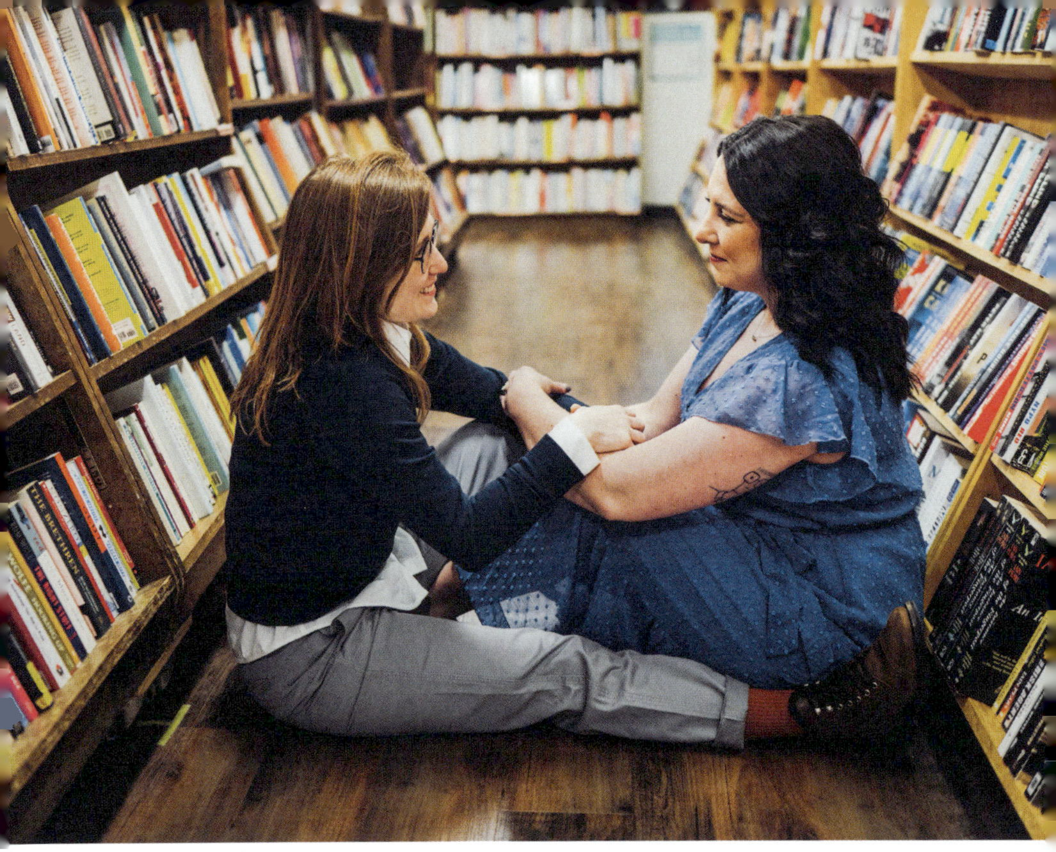

BREANNE AND NATALIE

Engaged: April 2, 2022 | Brookline Booksmith (Brookline, Massachusetts)

CLASSIC ROMANCE: Breanne and Natalie met online. After weeks filled with text messaging back and forth, they were eager to meet IRL and went to a movie theater for their first date. Unfortunately, not long afterwards, movie theaters and other businesses were forced to close, at least temporarily, due to Covid.

"During the pandemic," Breanne said, "we bonded over books. I told [Natalie] that my pandemic goal was to become a stronger reader and to start digging into the classics." At technical high school, Breanne hadn't had a chance to read many classics, and she felt as if she were missing out when people talked about the books that they had read.

Natalie loved helping Breanne with her reading project. Together the pair would roam through Brookline Booksmith's Used Book Cellar looking for classic reads like Ray Bradbury's *Fahrenheit 451*, Aldous Huxley's *Brave New World*, and Lois Lowry's *The Giver*.

When Breanne and Natalie got engaged,

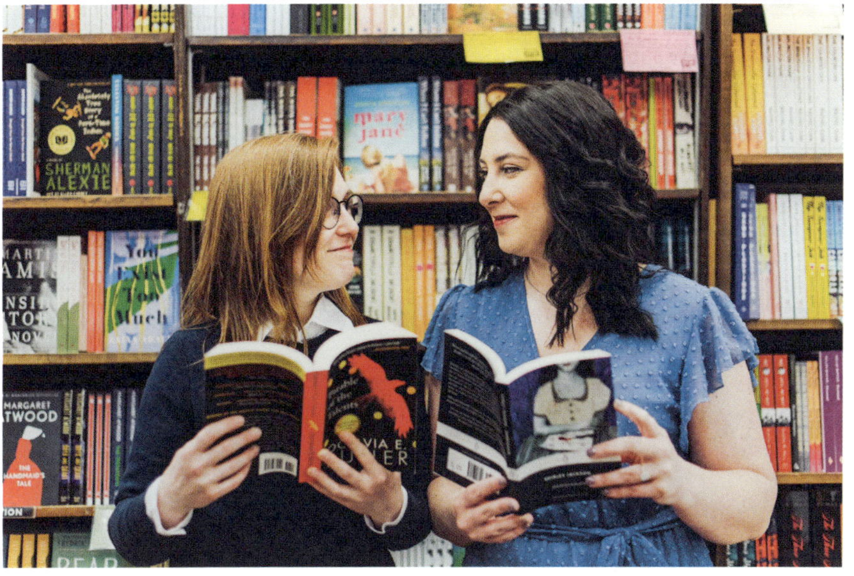

they wanted to commemorate those happy moments at Brookline Booksmith with photos.

Their choice clicked with their photographer Amanda Macchia. "When I book a session with a couple, I like to encourage them to be unique. I have a questionnaire that helps me to get to know them." In this case, Breanne and Natalie told Macchia that they both love books, reading, and graphic novels. "I said absolutely. I'm a book lover, too."

Their photographs seem so warm and and alive with love for each other and for the place where they've spent so many happy hours. This is due in part to Amanda's approach. "I'm in the business of celebrating warm and fuzzies. It keeps me humbled and excited to create these incredible memories for Natalie and Breanne."

At their wedding, Natalie and Breanne didn't skimp on books either. They chose a magical theme, and the centerpieces included navy and gold books covered in moss along with crystals, smudge sticks, and tarot card table markers. This time they had fun choosing books based on appearance rather than content.

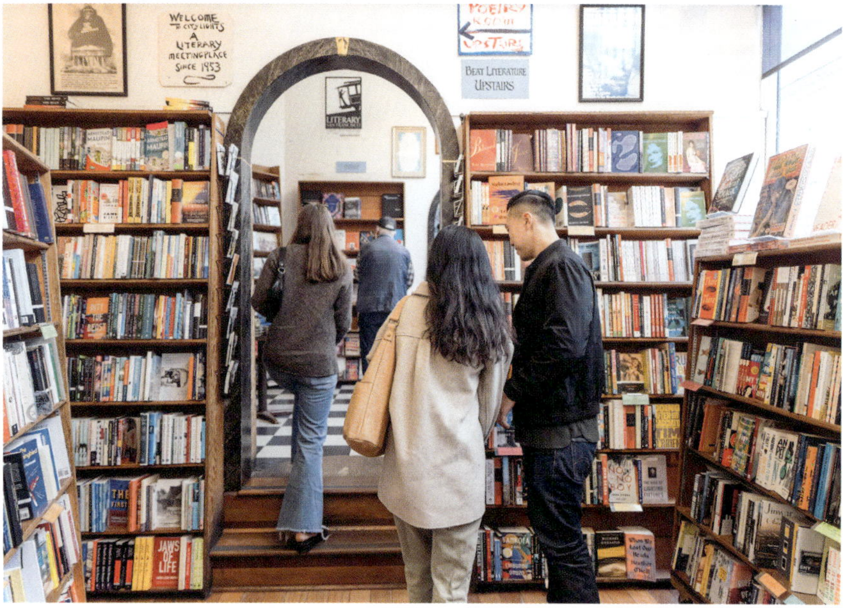

JENNIFER AND WARREN

Engaged: May 26, 2023 | City Lights Bookstore (San Francisco, California)

BOOKSTORES FOREVER! Jennifer loves bookstores so much, and Warren so loves taking her to them, that they never pass up a chance to visit.

"If we see a bookstore, we will always stop in, no matter what our initial plans were," Jennifer said. "We could be grocery shopping in a city for a destination vacation, and if there is a bookstore nearby, Warren would always ask me if I would like to go inside, even if we are in a time crunch."

Early in their relationship, Jennifer recalled going with Warren to pick up a prescription in Oakland. There was a small bookstore nearby, and he asked if she wanted to visit it. She did. So, they went in, and she got a book and a bookmark that she still uses.

Knowing that Jennifer's ideal date is, and always will be, visiting a bookstore, Warren wanted to incorporate a bookstore into his wedding proposal. But to make it a surprise, he told her that they were going to a sushi-making class.

Since City Lights was near "the class," he said that he needed to pick up a book there first. Jennifer didn't think anything of it. But

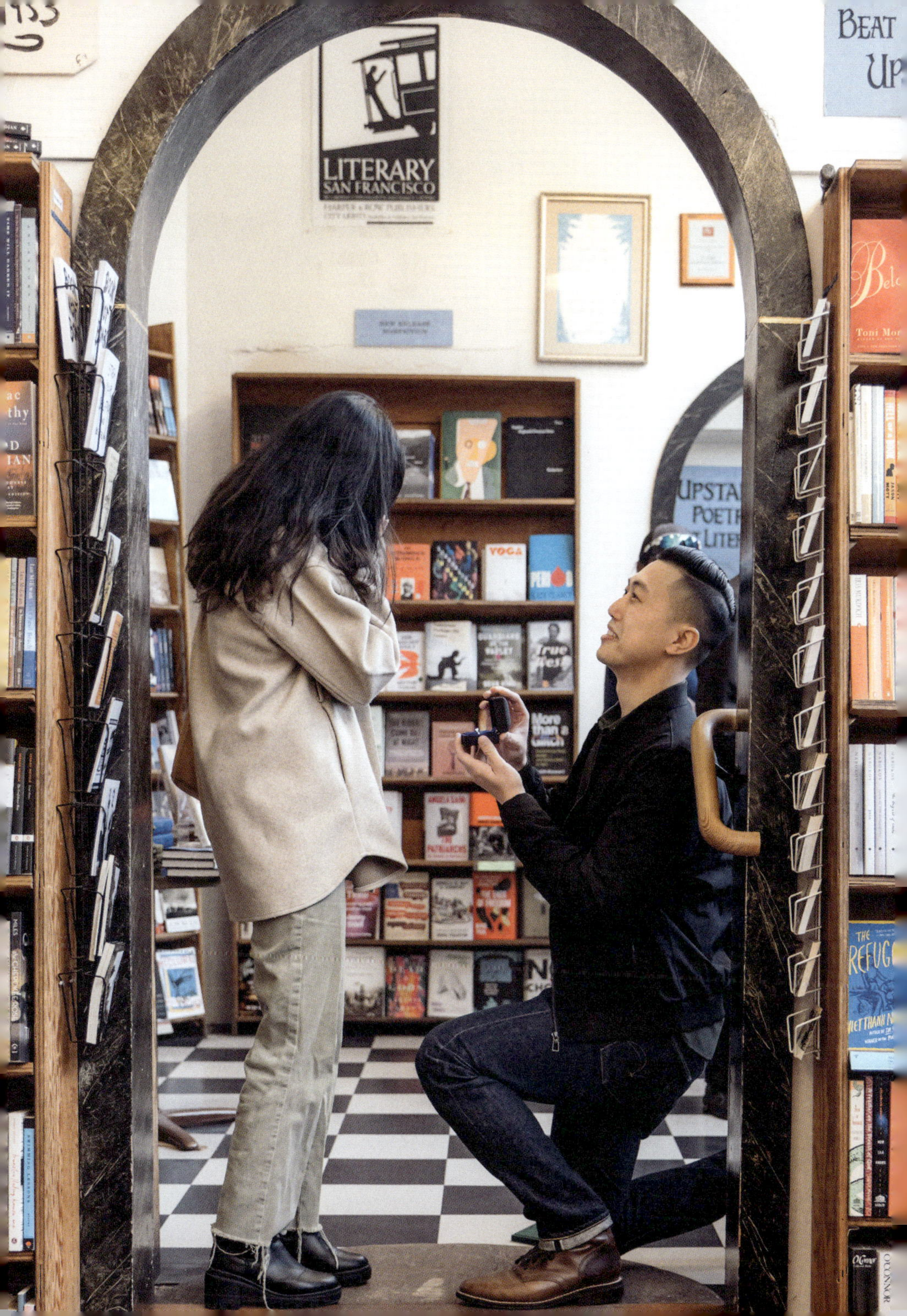
LITERARY
SAN FRANCISCO

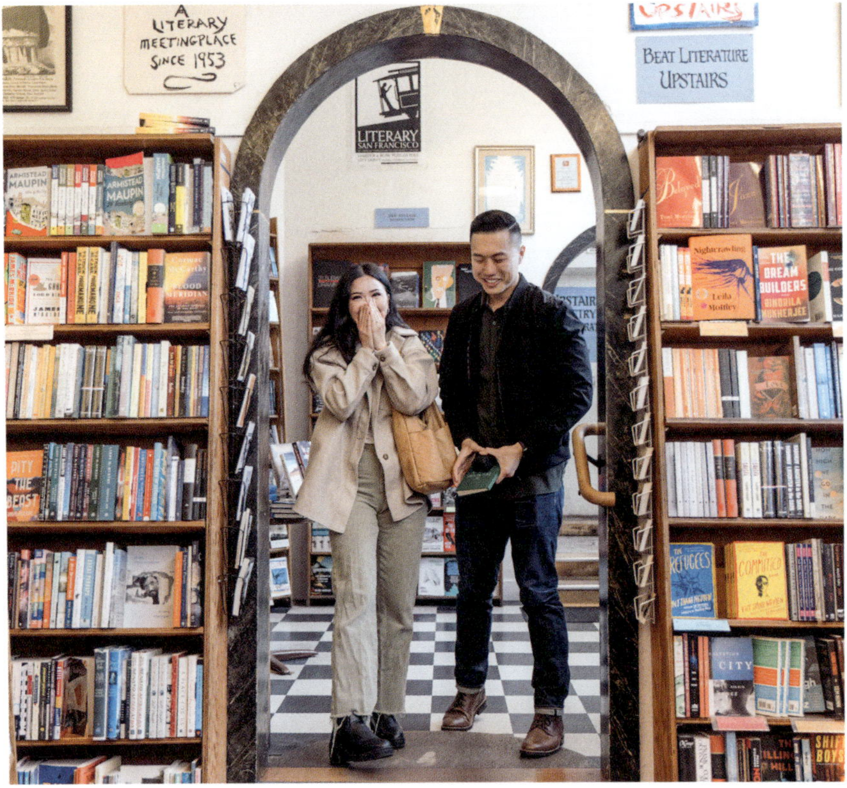

once they got inside, that changed when she realized that a camera crew was trailing behind her. And everyone in the store, both employees and customers, seemed to have "suspicious smiles on their faces."

Then Warren led her to the arch doorway where she saw their book. The title, *Two Moons and Back*, comes from a private joke from their first road trip to Paso Robles, and she realized what he was planning.

"I blacked out at this moment as he was speaking," she said, "and next thing you know, he was down on one knee with a gorgeous ring. I said, 'Yes,' right away." Then the store erupted with cheering and clapping.

In keeping with the couple's love of books, Warren and Jennifer are planning a book-and-nature-styled outdoor wedding with plenty of books, candles, and plants at the ceremony and reception. Their save-the-date cards will be vintage library book themed, and there will, of course, be bookmarks. Jennifer is also thinking about adding a few more bookish touches, including a book backdrop with a book-themed seating chart.

FRIDAY I'M IN LOVE:

DATE NIGHT AT THE BOOKSTORE

POST-COVID, PEOPLE STILL MEET CUTE AND GO ON DATES at bookstores and bookstore cafes. But for those who would like to find someone special and prefer to bypass dating apps, an increasing number of bookstores are stepping up to help.

Forty-year-old Trident Booksellers & Cafe in Boston's Back Bay works with Skip the Small Talk, a local organization, to run its speed-dating events, including registering the roughly thirty to forty people who sign up to participate each week. Though speed dating is typically aimed at those in their twenties and thirties, everyone is welcome. One week the bookstore schedules a general monogamous speed-dating event; the following week might target those looking for a bi and pan, or ace-spectrum bi-and-pan, partner. The store also hosts LGBTQIA+ speed-friending events.

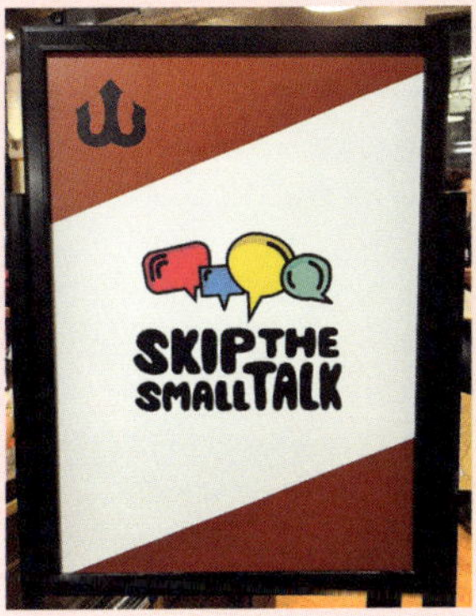

"Part of the appeal for bookstores like Trident," said co-owner Courtney Flynn, whose parents opened the bookstore and cafe in 1984, "[is that] there are few places to meet people by happenstance. And books are a natural conversation starter."

For those already in a relationship, who are looking to take the next step, Trident, which serves food and alcohol, recently created a room on the second floor specifically for wedding-adjacent events, ranging from breakfasts to bridal showers. The bookstore also hosts small weddings.

Philadelphia-based nonprofit publisher and community bookstore The Head & The Hand was looking to expand after pivoting to bookselling from publishing in 2019, just before the start of the Covid pandemic. So five nights per week, Wednesday through Sunday, H&H rents out the entire store for two ninety-minute slots, one slot per couple. Editorial director Linda Gallant credits her business partner Claire Moncla for coming up with the idea of Date Night, or "Friday I'm in Love," as it is known on the store's Instagram.

Date Night has been so successful that H&H recently scaled back its publishing program to three chapbooks per year. Part of the appeal for couples in diverse relationships is that the space is only eight hundred

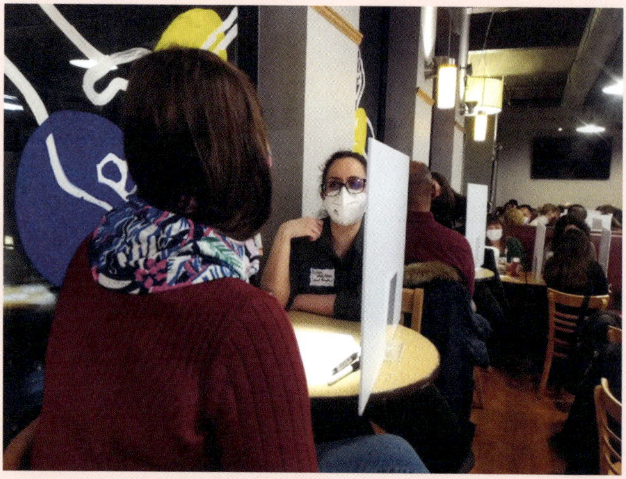

Scenes from Speed Dating with Books at Trident Booksellers & Cafe in Boston, Massachusetts.

square feet. "[It has] the vibe of a living room in a home away from home," Gallant said, adding that the store offers couples representing different types of love a place to go.

Several couples have gotten engaged at Date Night, according to Gallant. Aakash Patel's proposal to Neha Atyam was featured in the *Philadelphia Inquirer*. "Will you marry me?" Patel had written on a sign that Atyam couldn't miss when she entered the store for their agreed upon date. When she left, Atyam, who said "Yes," was wearing the ring that Patel had given her when he proposed on one knee with the soundtrack of "Good Days" by SZA in the background. She also had a new book to read.

At some stores speed dating is meant to bring people together over a good book. That's the case at Tombolo Books in St. Petersburg, Florida, which also opened in late 2019. "For the last two years we've celebrated Speed Dating with Books with gusto," events coordinator Kelsey Jagneaux said. She credits children's buyer Amanda Hurley with the idea of translating "rep picks" (typically done by publishers' representatives at book conventions for booksellers) into an event for bookstore customers who want to learn about new and upcoming books in the same rapid-fire succession.

The bookstore started Speed Dating with Books in conjunction with its Bookstore Romance Week celebration in August 2022. Local romance authors, book club leaders, and booksellers make the presentations, and everyone goes home with a free book, usually their first choice from among the presentations.

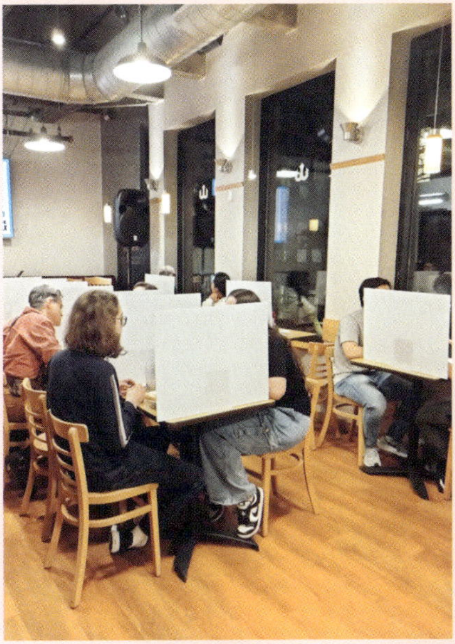

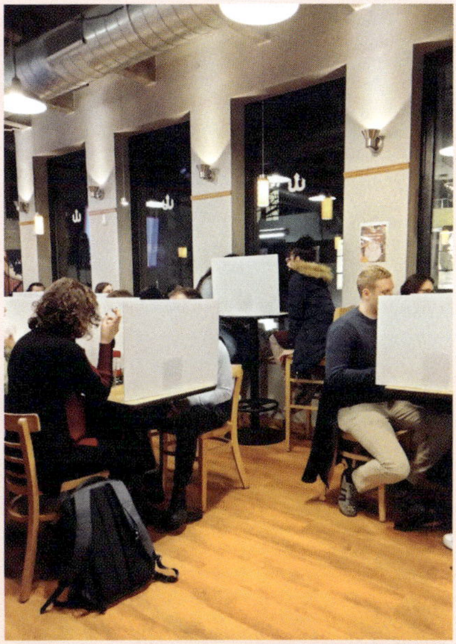

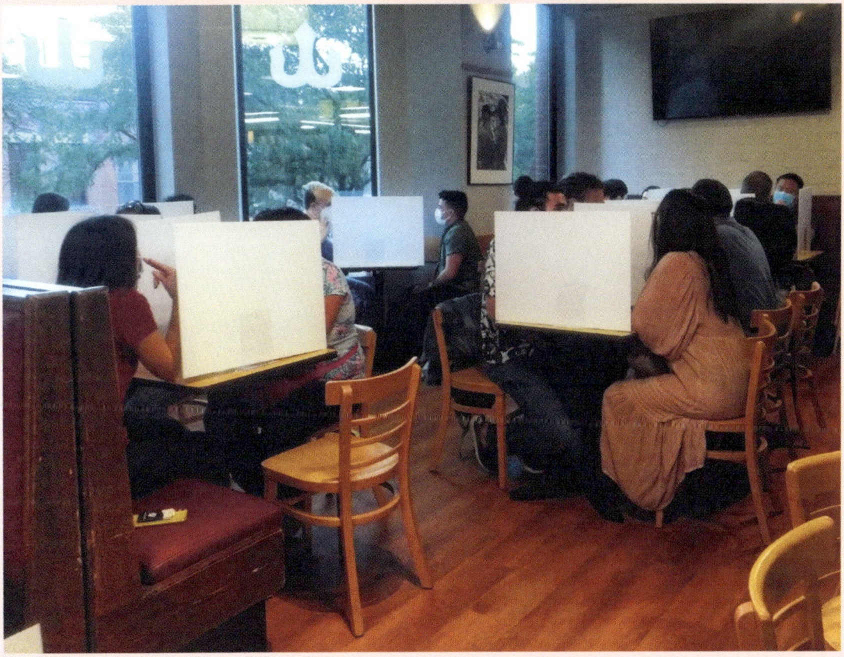

ALEXA AND DAVID

Engaged: August 19, 2023 | City Lit Books (Chicago, Illinois)

WILL YOU MARRY ME?: For David, proposing to Alexa on Bookstore Romance Day was "serendipity." He had purchased the ring months in advance and was waiting for the right moment.

The best weekend for friends and family to celebrate with them in Chicago coincided with the annual end-of-summer bookstore event. After Alexa nearly wrecked the surprise by accidentally seeing David's email exchange with City Lit, he pretended that the plan was ruined. He told her that they would have to get engaged another time, maybe in the fall.

To make the proposal really special, David had also begun working with a designer to craft a fake romance novel cover resembling the ones Alexa likes to read. It even had the same type of illustrations found on books by her favorite authors, Ali Hazelwood and Emily Henry.

The cover of David's book had line drawings of Alexa, himself, and their dog, Ozzie.

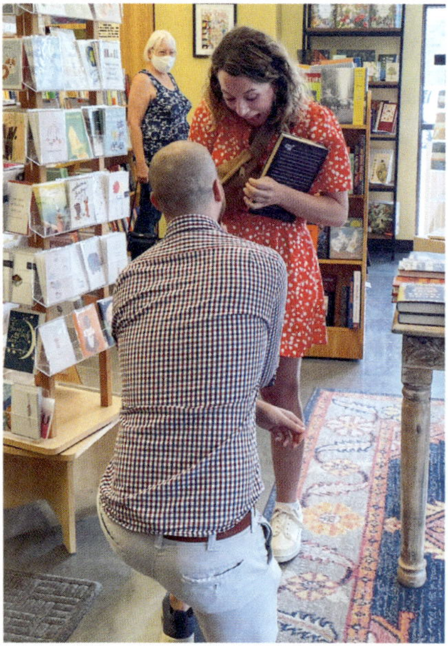

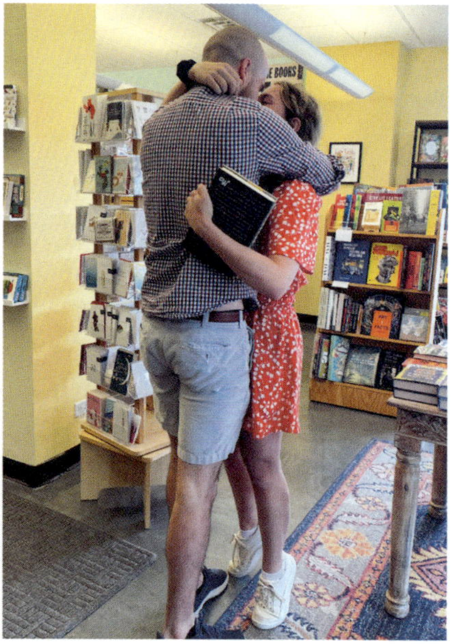

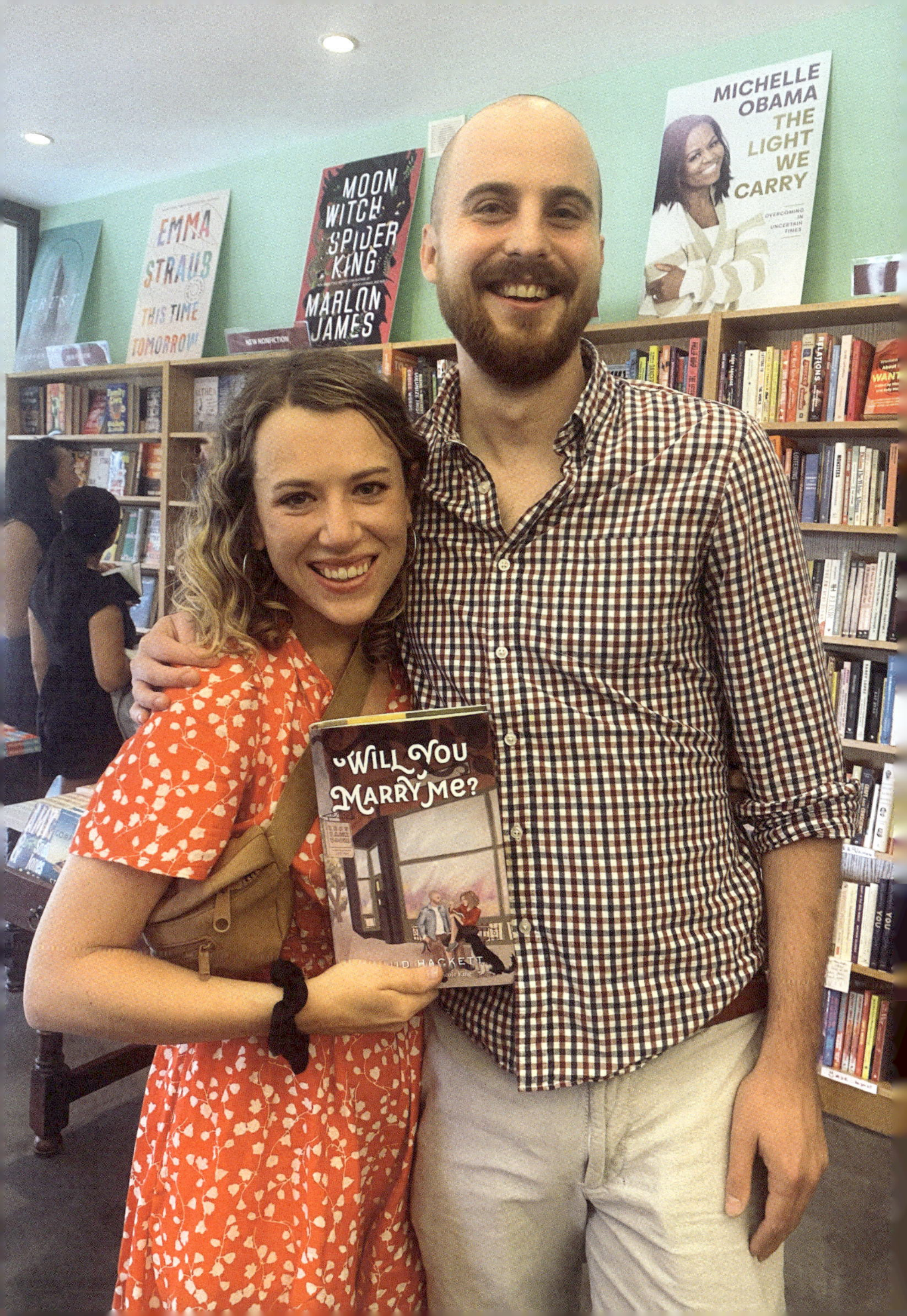
MICHELLE OBAMA
THE LIGHT WE CARRY
MOON WITCH SPIDER KING
MARLON JAMES
EMMA STRAUB
THIS TIME TOMORROW
WILL YOU MARRY ME?

As for the title, *Will You Marry Me?*, it was the question that had been foremost in his mind for a long time. But the trio on the cover weren't sitting in front of their favorite Chicago bookstore, City Lit, where the proposal was set to take place. Instead, the cover designer chose the bookstore that helped shape the couple's lives together, Left Bank Books in St. Louis. That's where Alexa and David had their second date, on the same day that they had their first kiss.

> *Alexa nearly wrecked the surprise by accidentally seeing David's email exchange with City Lit*

Alexa was genuinely surprised by the marriage proposal. David had arranged for friends to bring the book to the store before they got there. That way he was able to pick up the book at the front desk, while she was browsing as she usually did when she stopped by the store. But nothing seemed usual when she looked up and he handed her the book. Then he got down on one knee to ask the question.

Despite all of his careful planning, David forgot one thing, a photographer. Assistant bookstore manager Charlie Schumann stepped in to take pictures with a phone.

For their wedding, David and Alexa plan to return to St. Louis, where they met, and to get married at Left Bank Books. "[It] really holds a special place in our hearts and will forever be one of our favorite bookstores no matter where we live," David said.

A proposal at one favorite bookstore followed by a wedding at another? Now that's truly idyllic.

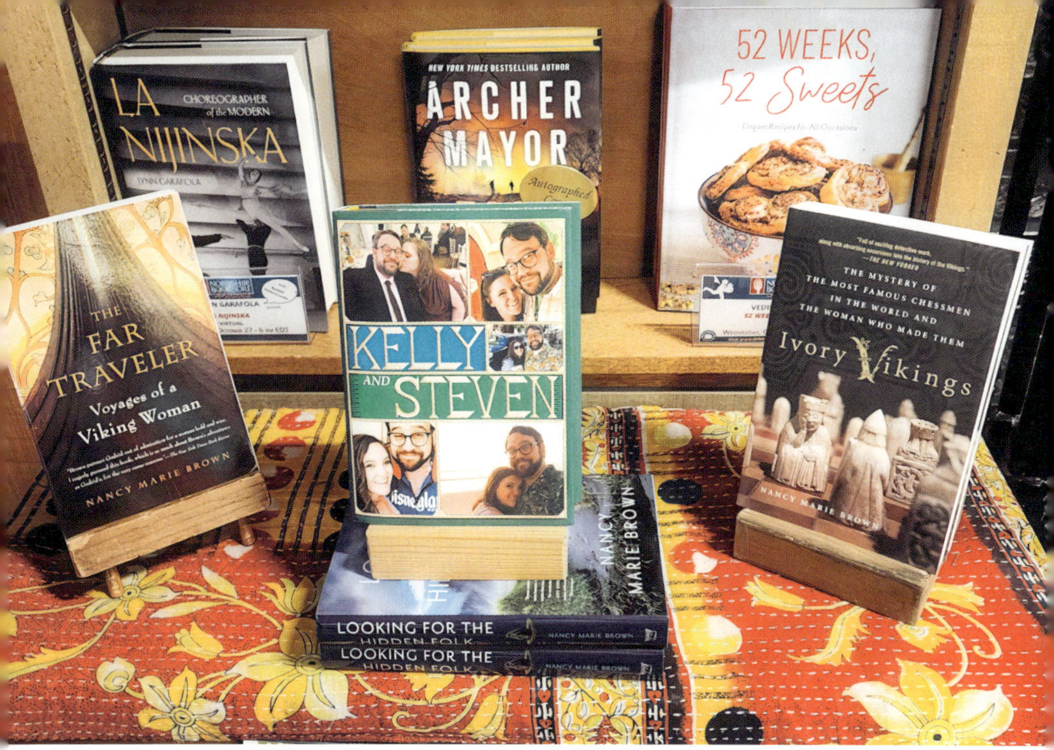

KELLY AND STEVEN

Engaged: October 6, 2022 | Northshire Bookstore (Manchester Center, Vermont)

SLEEPLESS IN NEW YORK: Kelly and Steven met at the Empire State Building Observatory, where he worked and where she was visiting from Florida with mutual friends. This may not have been exactly like Meg Ryan and Tom Hanks meeting there in *Sleepless in Seattle*, but Kelly and Steven felt a big enough spark to explore a long-distance relationship.

Their first official date was March 28, 2019, when he flew down to Orlando. By the time she visited him in New York City in May, he already knew about her "proclivity for all things reading," he said. So, he planned a trip to some of his favorite bookstores, including The Strand in New York City and Northshire Bookstore in Vermont, which he and his family visited every summer on their way to Lake Carmi.

Clearly, bookstore wooing worked. A year later Kelly found a job in New York City and moved in with Steven. Because of the pandemic, the pair went from navigating a long-distance relationship to being quarantined together.

By spring 2022, Steven knew that Kelly was the one and that Northshire was where he wanted to propose to his bookish girlfriend. For the ring, his mother gave him his Great-Great-Aunt Bessie's heirloom engagement

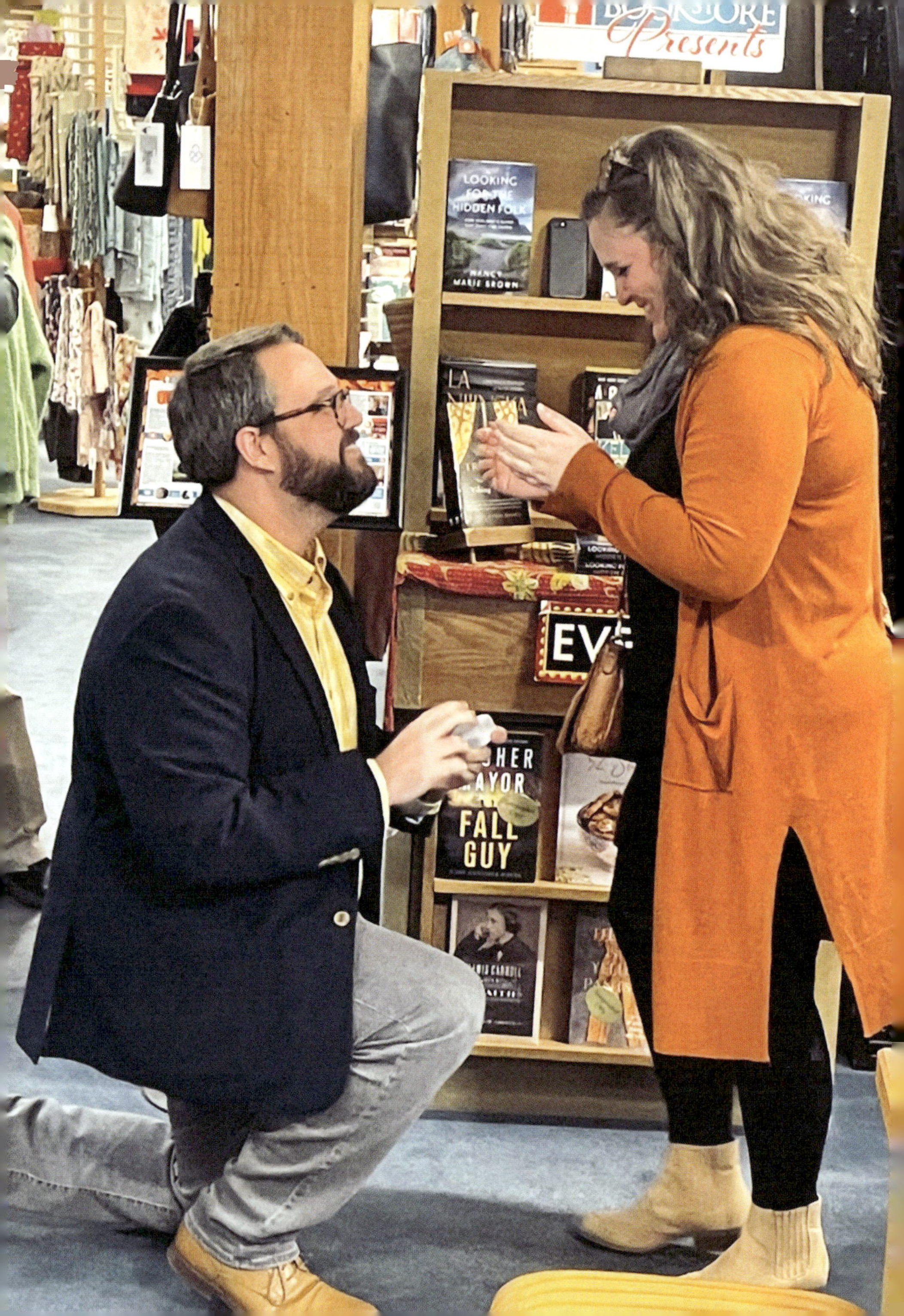
Presents
LOOKING FOR THE HIDDEN FOLK
NANCY MARIE BROWN
FALL GUY

ring, which is more than one hundred years old. He found a hollow book box on Etsy that he planned to use to tell his and Kelly's story. Knowing how much she liked the MinaLima design of the *Harry Potter* books, he asked a cousin, who is a designer, to create a book cover in that style and to decorate it with photos of Kelly and him together.

"It was a perfect moment. I would not have changed it for anything."

That summer Steven contacted Northshire to clear the date, and he asked Kelly's parents to come for a visit timed for the proposal. Then he planned for all of them to tour Vermont during leaf-peeping season. His own parents flew up from Florida to be there on the big day.

Once Kelly and Steven and his soon-to-be in-laws got to the bookstore, Kelly and her parents went inside. Steven went inside, too, and then went back to the car with a staffer, who brought the special book into the store. It had been hidden deep in one of the suitcases along with the ring. Once both sets of parents and the book were in place, Steven found Kelly and told her that there was a book that he wanted to show her.

The staffer had placed the *Kelly and Steven* book in a prime location on the first floor, with other books connected with Special Events. When she opened the book in surprise, he took out the ring. In the background, he recalled hearing a bookseller whisper, "I came back early from my break just to see this!"

Steven said to Kelly, "You know I love you, right?" Then he dropped to one knee and asked her to marry him. Later Steven said, "It was a perfect moment. I would not have changed it for anything."

The pair were married the following September in Vermont. Books were also an important part of their wedding, along with bourbon. Almost everything was made of book pages, Steven said, including bouquets of bookish flowers in Evan Williams and other bourbon bottles. Heart chains and pumpkins were also made from books. And there were even more books stacked up. For Kelly and Steven, there can never be too many books.

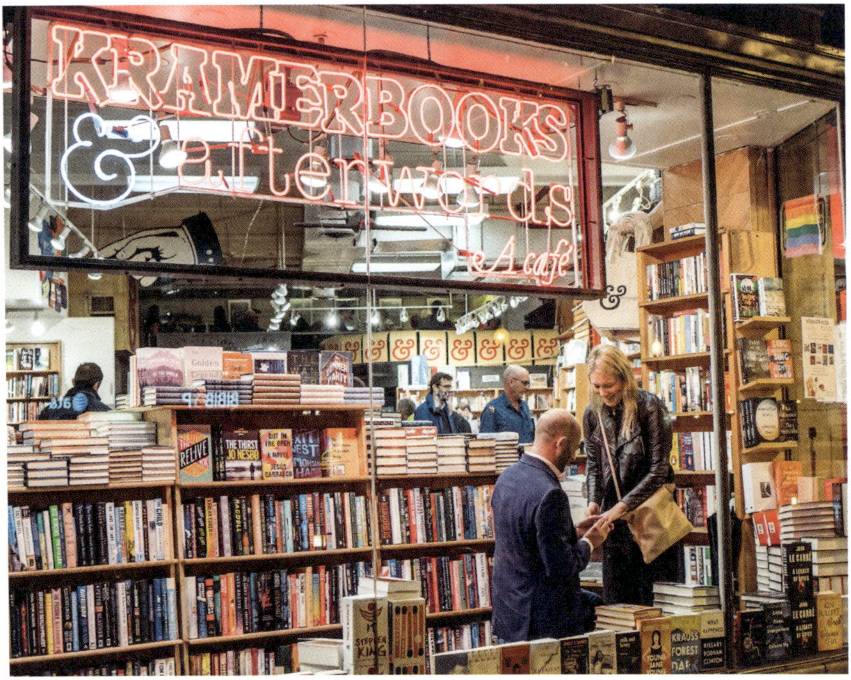

CLARE AND STEPHEN

Engaged: October 13, 2017 | Kramers (formerly Kramerbooks & afterwords café) (Washington, DC)

WRONG BOOK, RIGHT PARTNER: Stephen and Clare began dating after bonding over the wrong book. When the pair first met, Stephen knew he wanted to see her again and purchased a copy of a book that she had recommended so that they could talk about it. But when he got home and that very evening started reading, he realized by the end of the first chapter that Celeste Ng's *Everything I Never Told You* wasn't the book that she had described.

It turned out, however, to be exactly the book he needed as an excuse to give her a call right away to find out the name of the correct book. And as so often happens with book talk, one comment led to another. The pair quickly began dating, and suddenly Stephen was ready to propose on what he hoped would be a very lucky Friday the 13th.

He contacted Jen Capozzola, a photographer whom he and Clare both knew, and

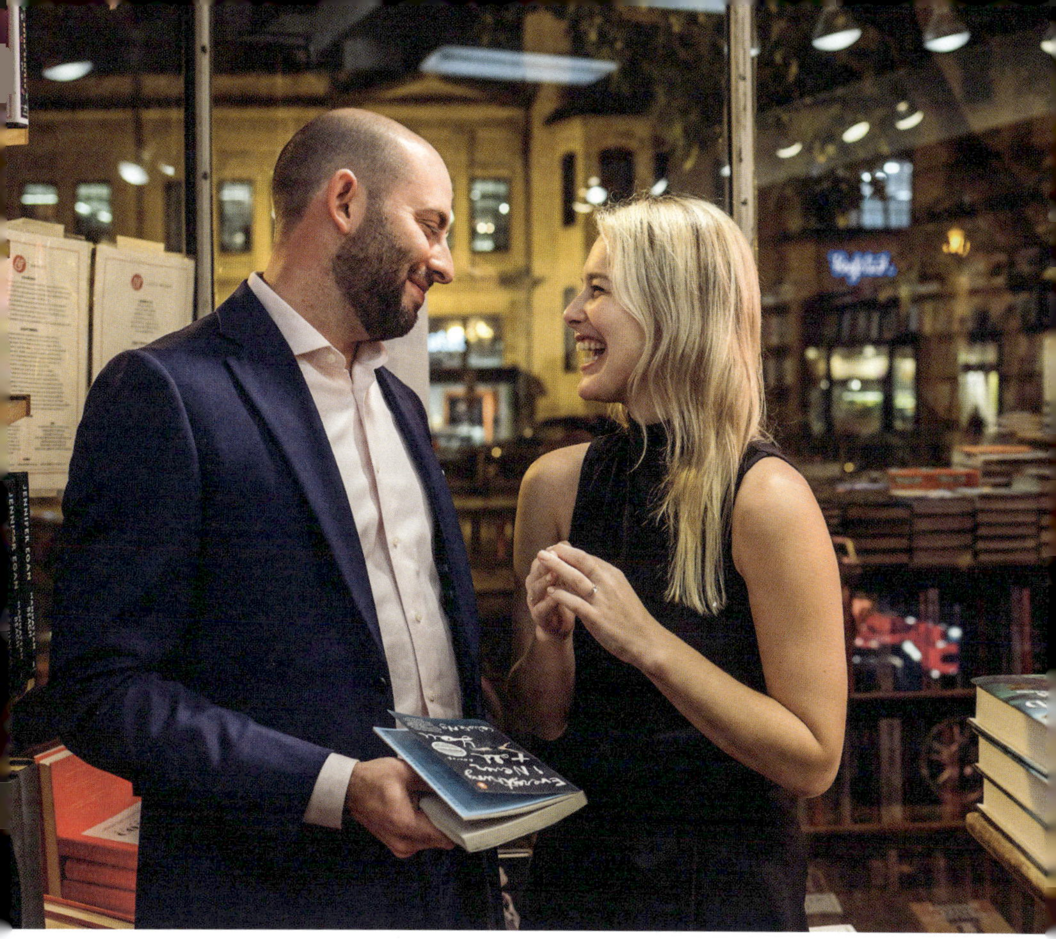

explained that he wanted to ask Clare to marry him at their favorite bookstore, Kramerbooks (now Kramers).

Although Jen scouts the locations where she's going to work in advance, Kramerbooks turned out to be more challenging than she had anticipated. In part that's because Stephen and Clare got held up in traffic and arrived an hour late, which meant it was much darker outside. In addition, to get the bookstore sign in the right direction for her photo, Jen had to stand outside the store and try to hide on Dupont Circle, while holding a camera.

A small crowd, who wanted to see the proposal, too, gathered around her, in front of the bookstore window. Fortunately, Clare only had eyes for Stephen and was completely surprised by the ring, which he had placed inside Ng's novel, and by the photographer.

Suddenly, there was nothing "wrong" about Ng's book. In fact, it was very right.

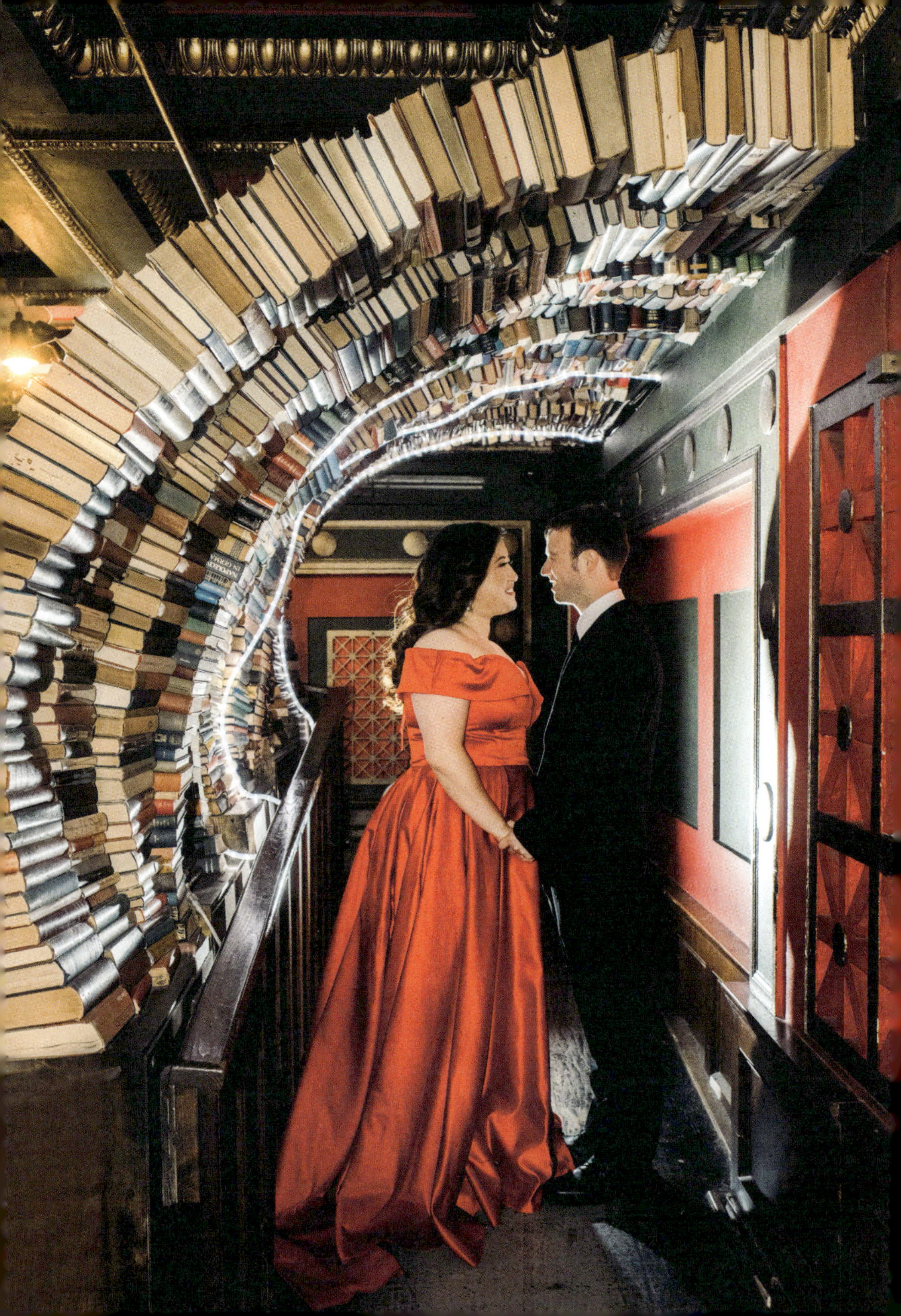

DRU AND KRISTEN

Engaged: November 25, 2019 | The Last Bookstore (Los Angeles, California)

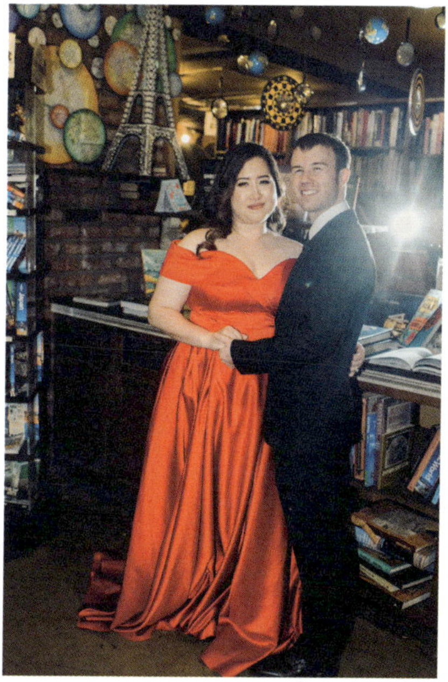

MARRIED TWICE: When Kristen met Dru at IndieCade, a video game conference, neither of them were looking for someone to date. She was there because she wanted to break into the video game industry. And he was working at the company where she was hoping to get hired. So she readily assented when Dru invited her to a bar where he and some of his colleagues would be hanging out.

But, after the festival ended, they continued to see each other, even though Dru told her he wasn't ready to date. These may have been what Kristen called "nondates," but that first one, for brunch and a visit at The Last Bookstore in downtown LA, clearly made a big impression on both.

As for breaking into the video game industry, Kristen eventually got hired by the same company as Dru, but without his help. He didn't want the appearance of a conflict of interest. And they overlapped for less than a year before he started his own company.

Kristen and Dru got engaged in Kyoto, Japan, but that first "nondate" was so important to them both that they chose to commemorate their engagement at The Last Bookstore. Kristen wore a beautiful red dress for the occasion. "I always wanted my Belle moment from *Beauty and the Beast*," she said, "to have my gown and a lot of books."

Both Dru and Kristen are huge fantasy fans. But the couple's first wedding wasn't very romantic. This took place at a courthouse in June 2020 behind Covid-prevention glass. It took another two years before they were able to hold their second wedding at the venue where they had originally planned to marry in 2020. By then, they were already the parents of a young child. So they ended up scrapping their original plans to introduce more fantasy into their wedding with *Lord of the Rings*, *Harry Potter*, *The Little Prince*, and *Winnie the Pooh* moments. But Kristen did walk down the aisle to "Concerning Hobbits" from the *Lord of the Rings* film.

Now that they've been married twice, Kristen said, the hard part has been choosing which wedding day to celebrate as their anniversary.

BRENDAN AND SAM

Engaged: September 26, 2021 | Old Town Books (Alexandria, Virginia)

WHEN BRENDAN MET SAM: Friends to lovers may be a classic romance trope. But first-responders Brendan and Sam began their relationship even earlier, as coworkers.

After the two became friends on the job, they ended up sharing a place to live. It was only then that they started dating.

One of the ways that Brendan won Sam over was by being easy to live with. Now that they're married, he said, she calls him a "turn-key husband."

Because Brendan knew that Sam is "an absolute bibliophile," he wanted to get engaged at a bookstore. When he was ready to propose, he chose her favorite store, Old Town Books in the Old Town section of Alexandria, Virginia. "It's a location she holds near and dear to her heart," he said. Sam belonged to a book club at Old Town and had become friends with bookstore owner Ally Kirkpatrick.

When Sam and Brendan married the following year, they chose the George Peabody Library in Baltimore, Maryland, for their venue. It is nicknamed the "Cathedral of Books." There the couple were surrounded by even more books, 300,000 of them.

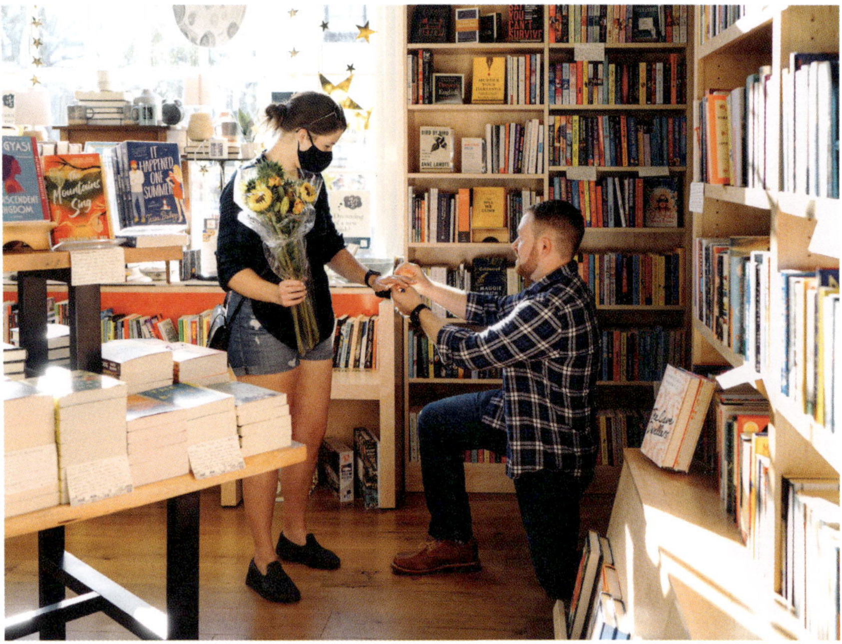

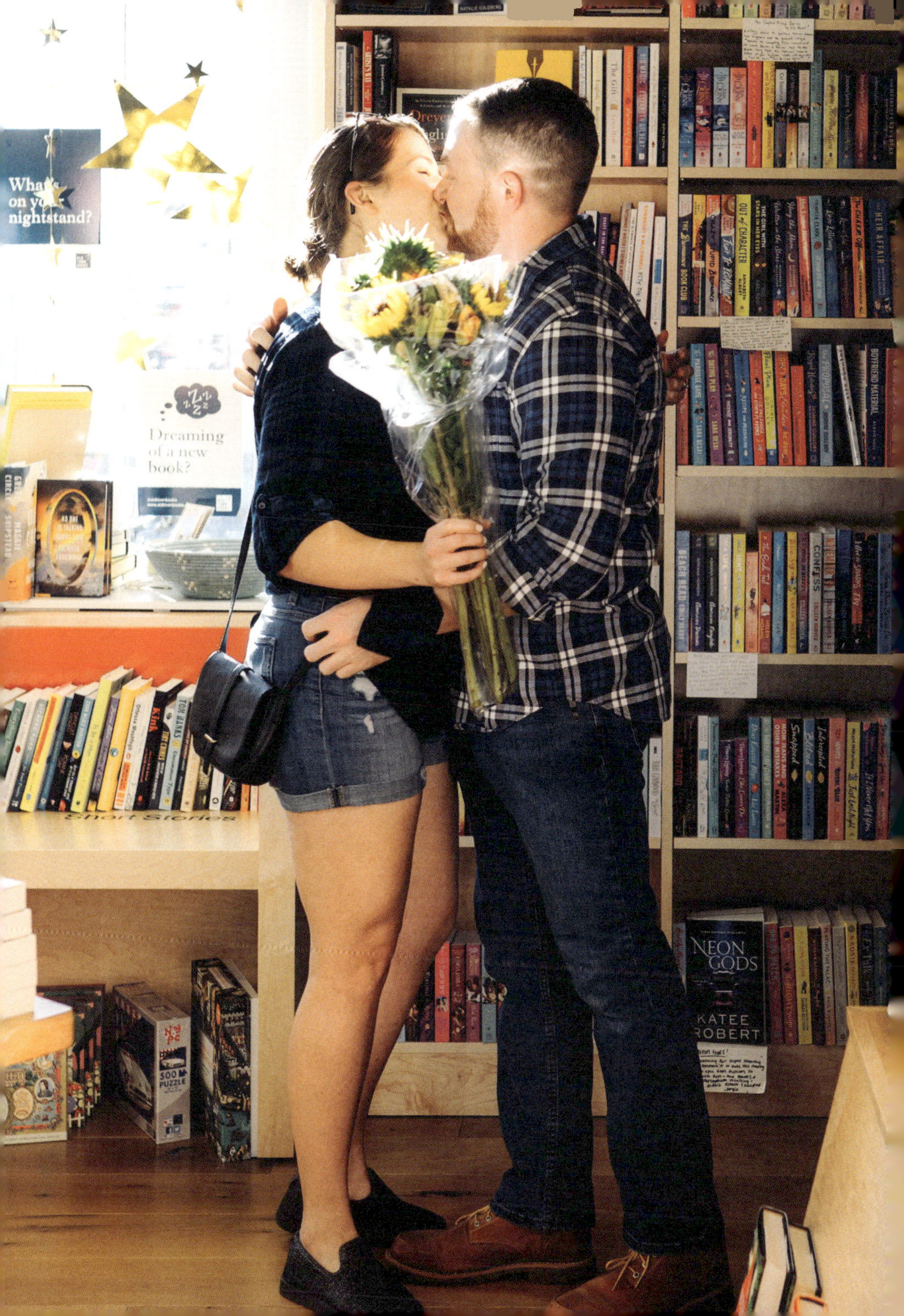

Dreaming of a new book?
NEON GODS
KATEE
Short Stories
500 PUZZLE

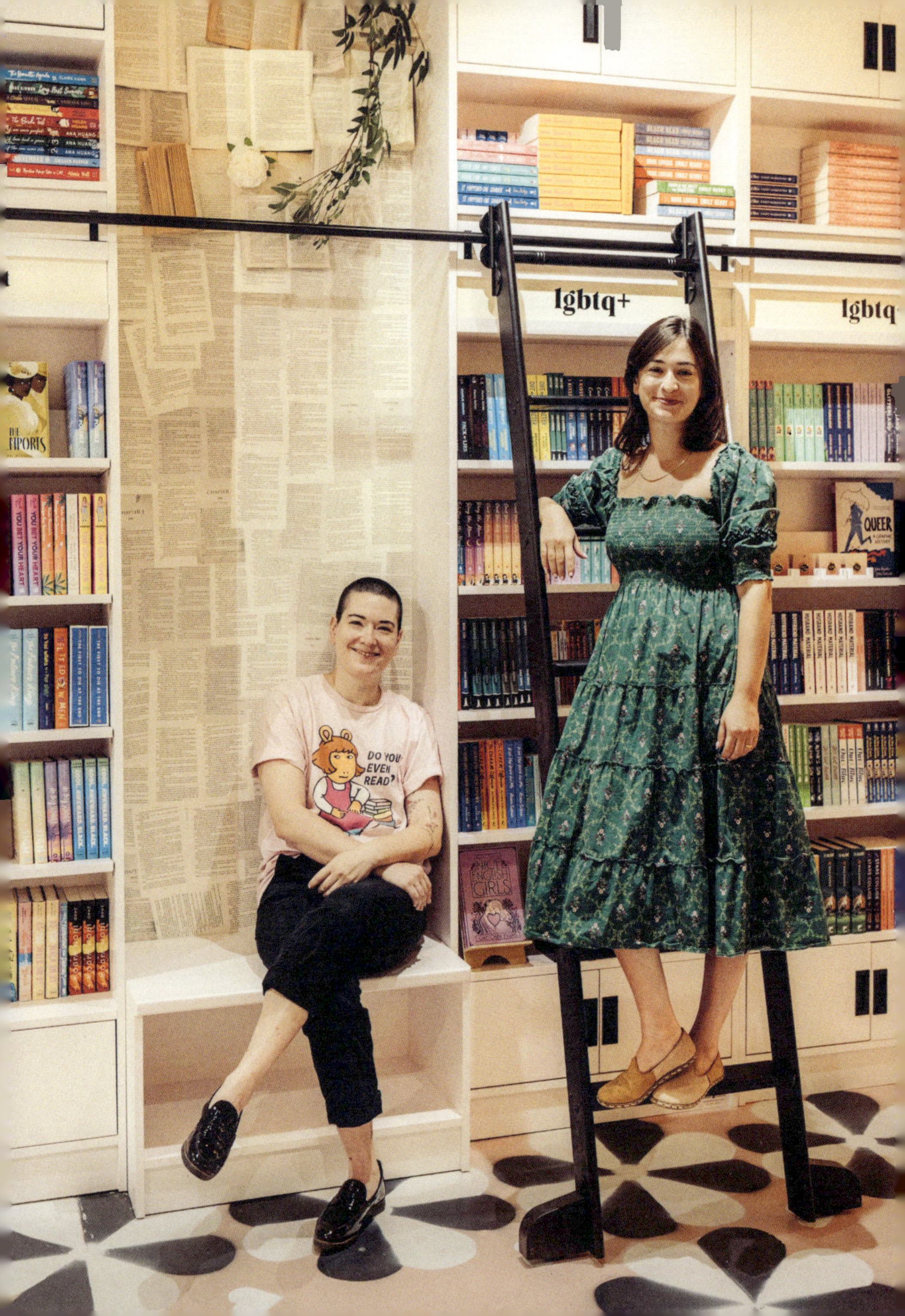
lgbtq+
lgbtq
DO YOU EVEN READ?
QUEER

WHERE ROMANCE COMES FIRST:

THE RIPPED BODICE

Sisters and bookstore owners Leah (*left*) and Bea (*right*) at The Ripped Bodice in Brooklyn, New York.

WHEN SISTERS BEA AND LEAH KOCH OPENED THE RIPPED Bodice in Culver City, California, a decade ago in 2016, there were many naysayers. Some wondered how a large bookstore devoted exclusively to romance could survive. Others questioned the name of the store itself, which is taken from an epithet for sexually explicit romance books, "bodice-rippers." This genre is also the focus of Bea's master's thesis, "Mending the Ripped Bodice."

Looking back, Leah said that she and Bea always knew that the store would be successful. "If we weren't 100 percent sure," Leah added, "I would have questioned why we were gambling a lot of money on this situation." Plus, they were able to expand, once the height of Covid was past, and began looking for a second location in the Park Slope section of Brooklyn, New York. When the new store opened on August 5, 2023, the line, which stretched from one avenue to the next all day long, exceeded even Leah's expectations.

In addition to expanding to a second location, other measures of The Ripped Bodice's success include an increase in employees from zero to seventeen and a steady stream of enthusiastic customers.

Close to two dozen other romance bookstores have opened in the intervening years, including in Salt Lake City; Wichita, Kansas; Minneapolis; and Cambridge, Massachusetts. One outlier that predates them all, Turn the Page Bookstore in Boonsboro, Maryland, opened in 1995 and features primarily books by a single romance author, Nora Roberts, aka J. D. Robb. That store's owner is her husband, Bruce Wilder.

Since Covid, The Ripped Bodice and other romance bookstores have benefited from a new genre—romantasy, a mixture of romance and fantasy—which was the word of the week at the 2022 Frankfurt Book Festival, where international rights to books are sold to publishers from around the world. That interest in the intersection of the two genres has continued in the intervening years, led by bestselling authors such as Sarah J. Maas and Rebecca Yarros, who are also popular on TikTok.

At The Ripped Bodice, Leah said, "Romantasy is definitely having a moment. But it depends on how deeply you want to delve, because contemporary romance has not really waivered. I think paranormal has gone up, and historical has gone down a little, but it's still always going to be popular." The stores' six major subgenres are: contemporary, historical, paranormal fantasy, erotica, YA, and LGBTQ+.

Rather than shifts in the popularity of specific categories, the biggest change that Leah has observed in romance recently is the age of her customers, which has dropped due to TikTok and the pandemic. In what she regards as "normal times," a number of people turn eighteen and age into reading romance. "In this case, because so many people were stuck at home, it was a much, much larger age span and influx all at once. I love talking to young people. They have been raised in a post-Amazon generation to understand that if they don't support independent bookstores they will be left with giant warehouses."

And, yes, there is romance at the bookstore. "It was the most exciting day of my life, when someone asked if they could propose at the store," Leah said. Since then, both stores have hosted proposals as well as bachelorette parties and bridal showers. But last year Leah had two even more swoon-worthy events, when both stores hosted their first weddings.

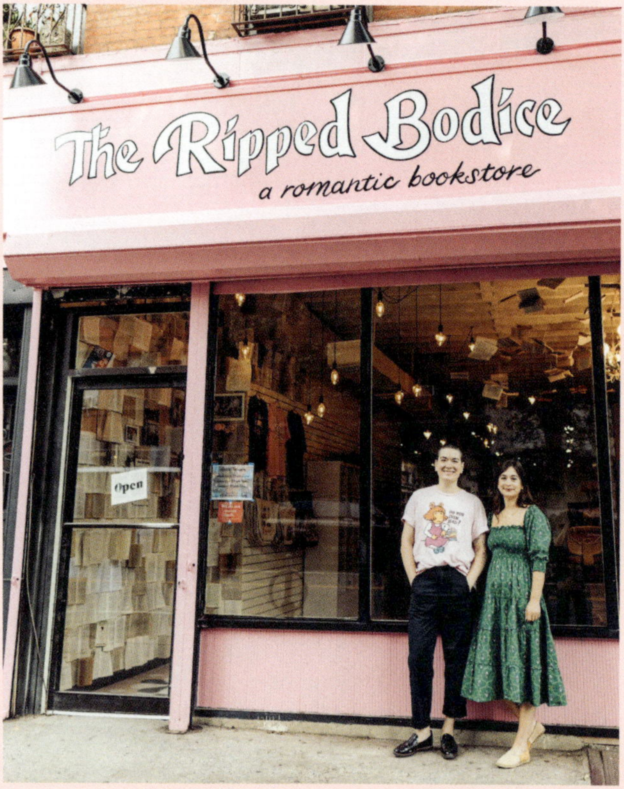

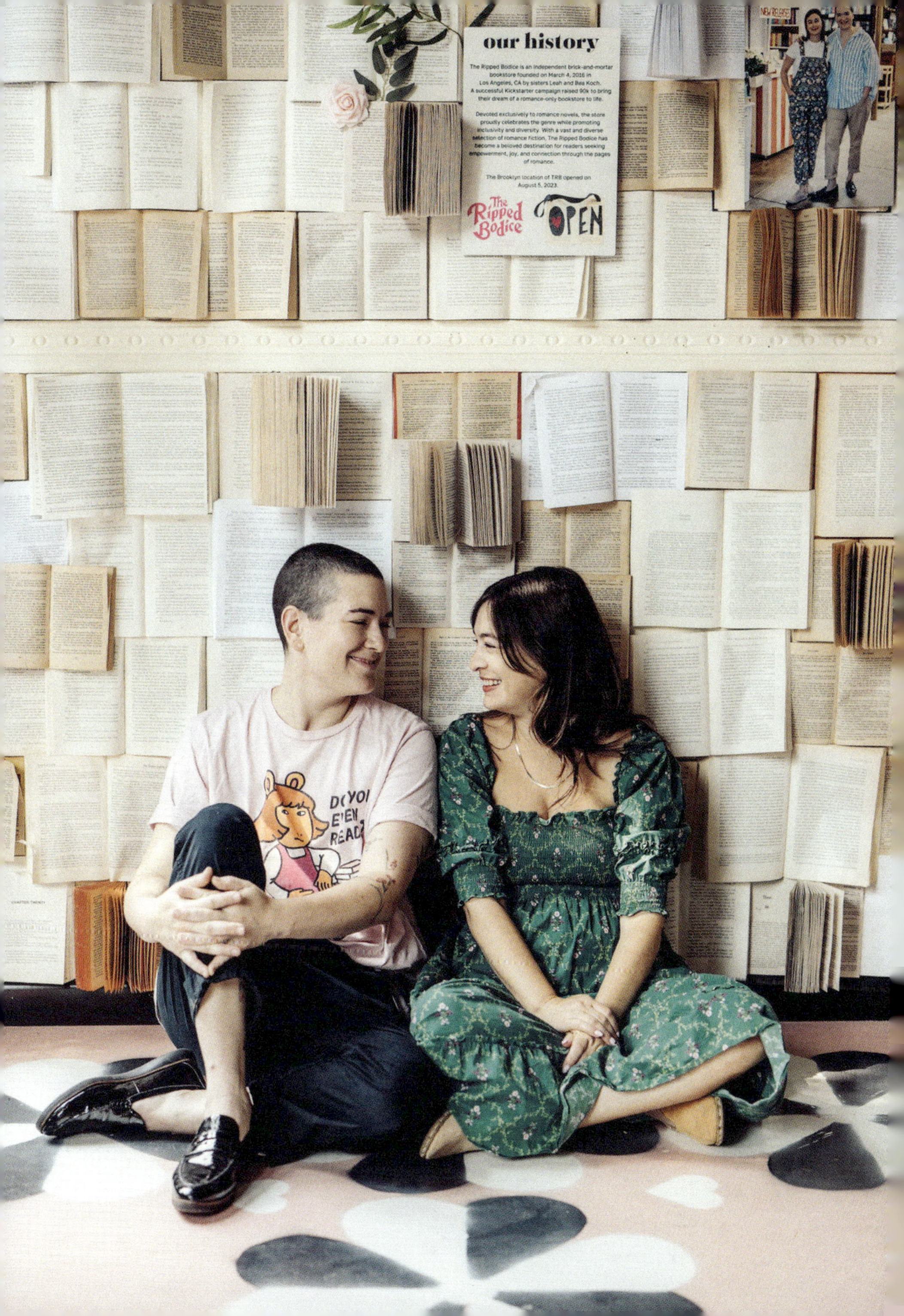
our history
The Ripped Bodice is an independent brick-and-mortar bookstore founded on March 4, 2016 in Los Angeles, CA by sisters Leah and Bea Koch. A successful Kickstarter campaign raised 90k to bring their dream of a romance-only bookstore to life.
Devoted exclusively to romance novels, the store proudly celebrates the genre while promoting inclusivity and diversity. With a vast and diverse selection of romance fiction, The Ripped Bodice has become a beloved destination for readers seeking empowerment, joy, and connection through the pages of romance.
The Brooklyn location of TRB opened on August 5, 2023.
The Ripped Bodice
OPEN
DO YOU EVEN READ?

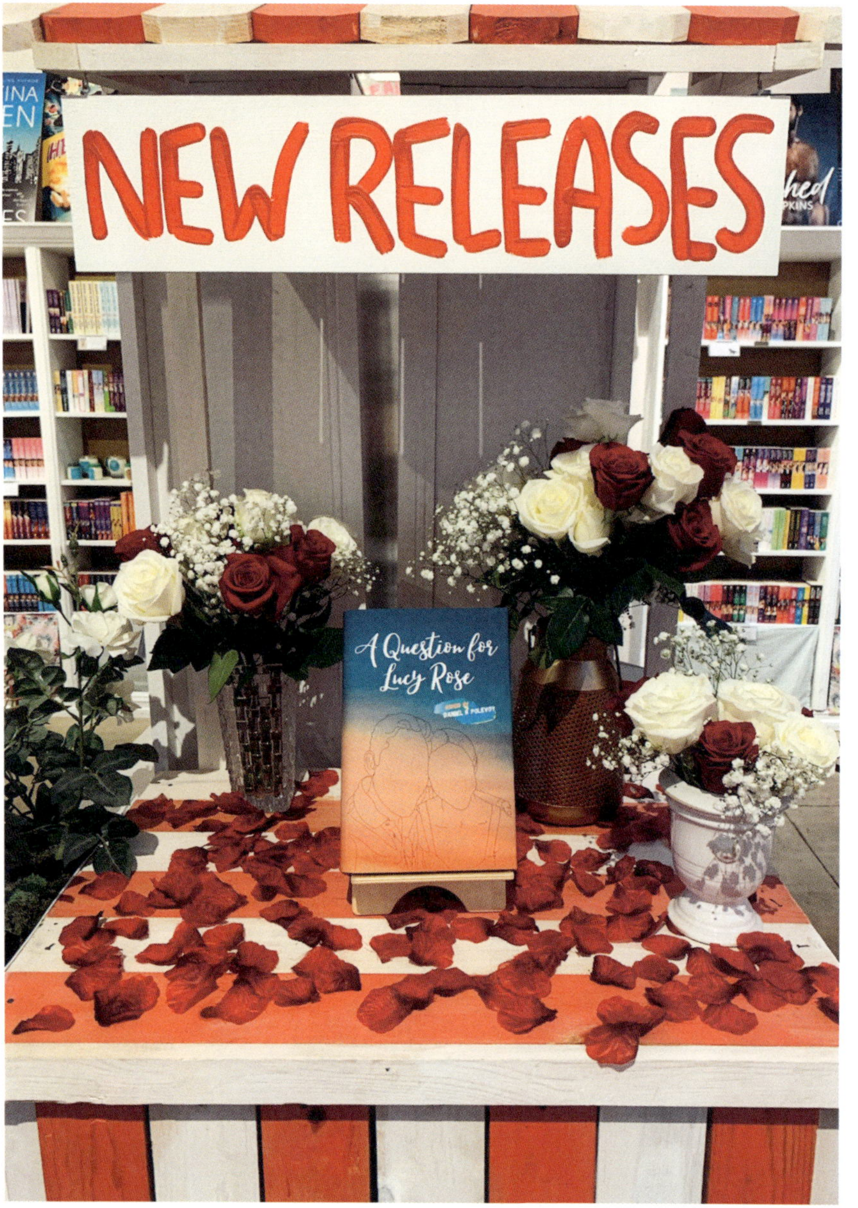
NEW RELEASES
A Question for Lucy Rose

DANNY AND LUCY

Engaged: February 24, 2022 | The Ripped Bodice (Culver City, California)

ISN'T IT ROMANTIC?: Danny and Lucy actually met twice before dating each other. The first time, which Danny doesn't remember, was at a party at Syracuse University where they were both in theater school. The second time, Lucy was performing in a show and Danny was working backstage.

Fast forward seven years. After dating in college and moving to Los Angeles together, Lucy and Danny were both ready to take their relationship further. But for Danny, the question became how to surprise the woman you love with a proposal, when she has already worked with a jeweler to design her engagement ring, the ring that she wants to wear for the rest of her life.

To keep Lucy guessing, Danny resorted to a technique often used in mysteries, planting a red herring to keep her off track. "I had planned a vacation to Hawaii for the following week, which is where I knew Lucy would be *convinced* I was proposing," Danny

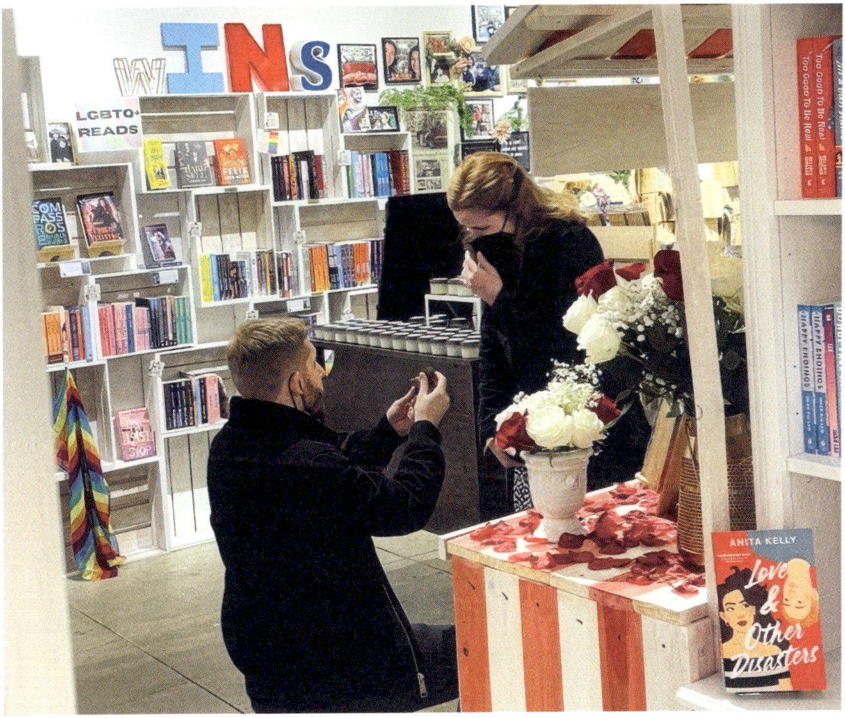

said. Instead, on the day after her birthday he lured her to a favorite bookstore, The Ripped Bodice, and offered to buy her a book there for the trip.

"I think the proposal was so special because it was built around something Lucy loves. Not only was I able to ask her to spend the rest of our lives together, but I did my best to express that I'm eager to support and share her passions," Danny said.

> To keep Lucy guessing, Danny resorted to a technique often used in mysteries, planting a red herring to keep her off track.

When they got to the bookstore, Lucy recalled feeling "magnanimous" by asking Danny if he would rather wait outside while she browsed. Instead, he suggested that she look at a book he thought that she would like on the New Releases table, *A Question for Lucy Rose*. The book was surrounded by roses, and he invited her to open it. When she did, she saw that it had a compartment he had hollowed out, which held a wooden ring box. He took the box out, knelt in front of her, and asked, "Will you marry me?"

Lucy's response was so soft that she heard someone else in the store ask, "Did she say, 'Yes?'" Then she heard store co-owner Leah Koch respond, "She said 'Yes!'"

But Danny wasn't finished with surprises. Two of the couple's best friends came out from behind the sales counter with fistfuls of rose petals, and Lucy burst into tears. When they all left the store, Lucy saw her and Danny's parents sitting outside a nearby coffee shop. Danny had arranged for them to fly in for the engagement. He had also arranged with her boss for her to have the next day off, so she could spend it with their families.

Although Lucy didn't get a book to read that day, she is very happy with the book Danny created for her. They even brought it to the wedding. "Now," she said, "it lives on a shelf in our living room, where everyone can see what a thoughtful, creative man I somehow convinced to marry me, and all my books."

Sometimes the second time is a charm.

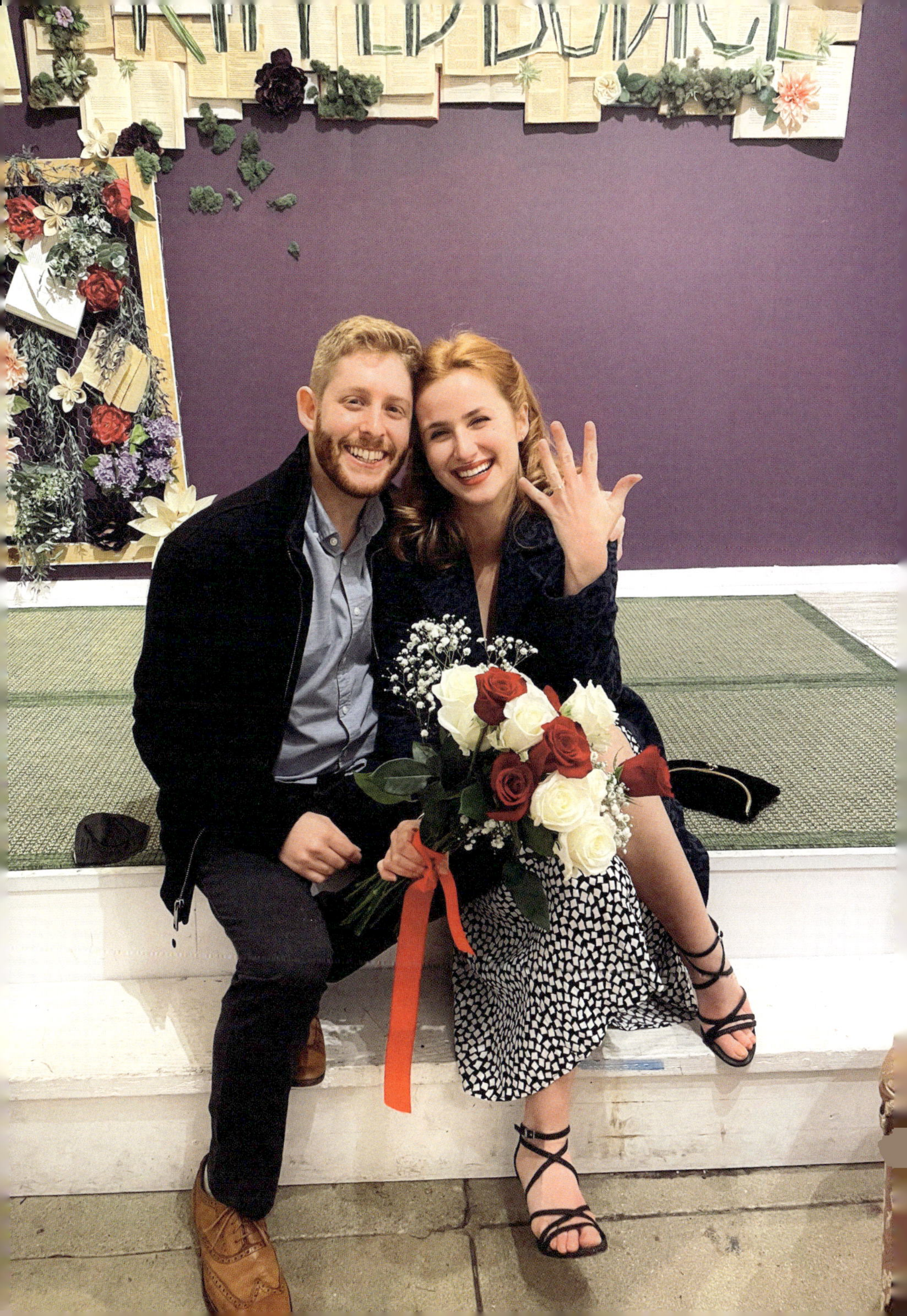

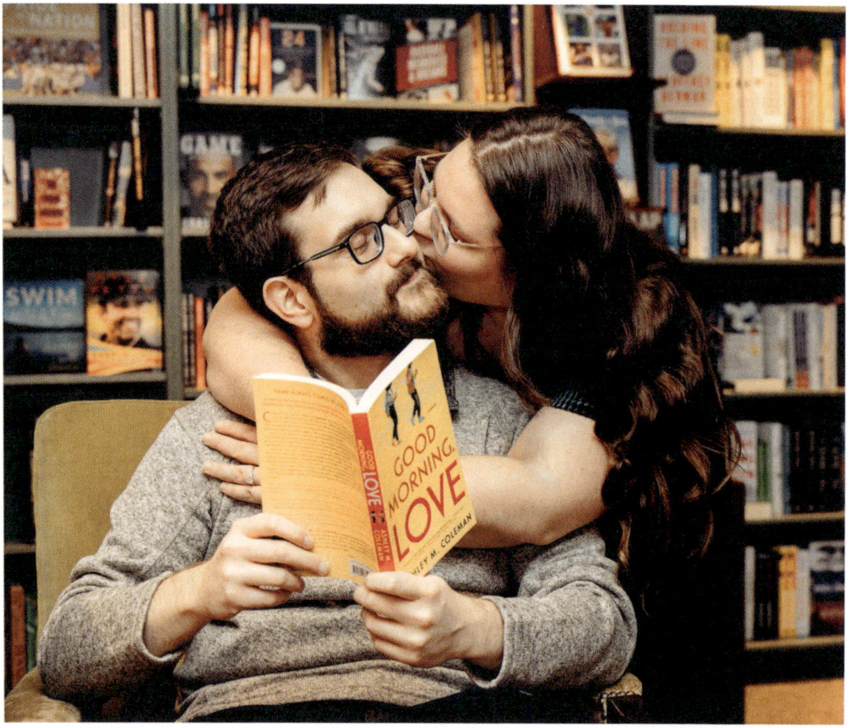

CAROLINE AND MICHAEL

Engaged: June 11, 2022 | RJ Julia Booksellers (Madison, Connecticut)

FIND YOUR STORY: When Michael met Caroline, it wasn't because she had made the first move on Bumble. It was actually her coworker who saw his profile on Caroline's phone and chose Michael on her behalf. But Caroline doesn't mind. Because clearly her coworker was right; the two of them are a perfect match.

For his marriage proposal, Michael planned a picnic at a lavender farm in Rhode Island, where they had one of their first dates. Six months later for the engagement photo session, the pair chose a different location, RJ Julia Booksellers, which also holds great significance for them.

This bookstore was Michael's local independent growing up, the place where he picked out the books he needed for school and continues to find reading material. And he introduced it to

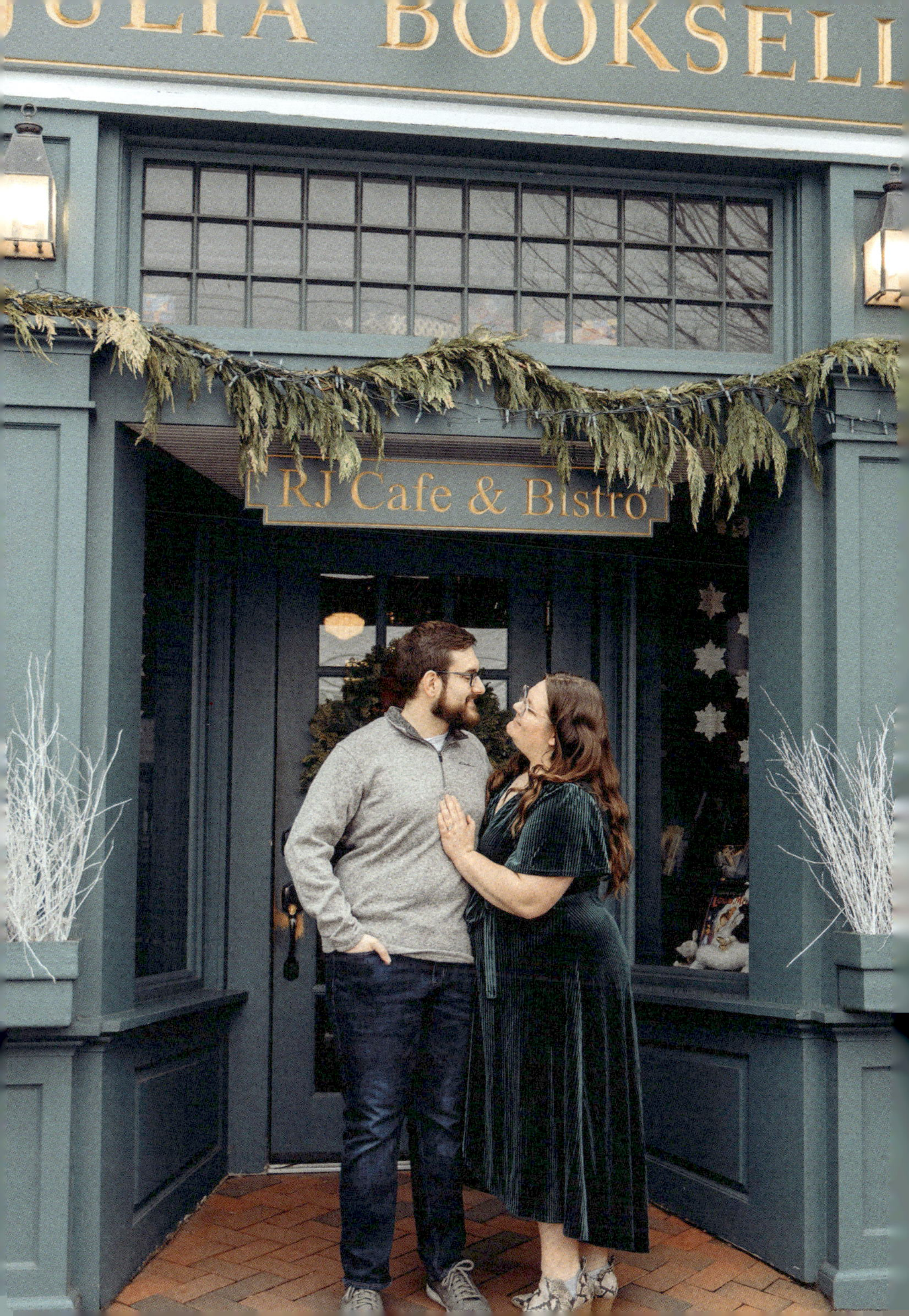
RJ Cafe & Bistro

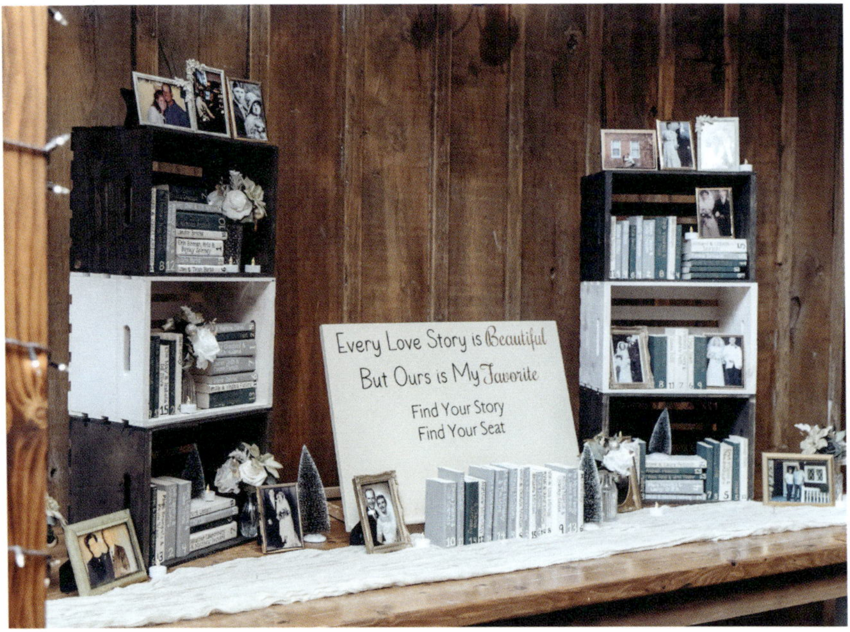

Caroline, a self-described "bookstore person," who likes to read widely. The store quickly became one of her favorites, too.

"We're very sentimental about small things," Caroline said. That even extends to a book that they specifically chose for their engagement photos, Emily Stone's *Always, in December*. By then, the pair were already planning to say their "I do's" on December 3.

Books were carefully chosen for the wedding as well. "Caroline always figures out something lovely, and sentimental," Michael said, admiringly. Instead of an ordinary seating chart, Caroline made bookcases from wooden crates and filled them with fake books with the names of the guests and their table numbers on the spines. Family wedding photos were also on display, along with a sign: "Find your story, find your seat."

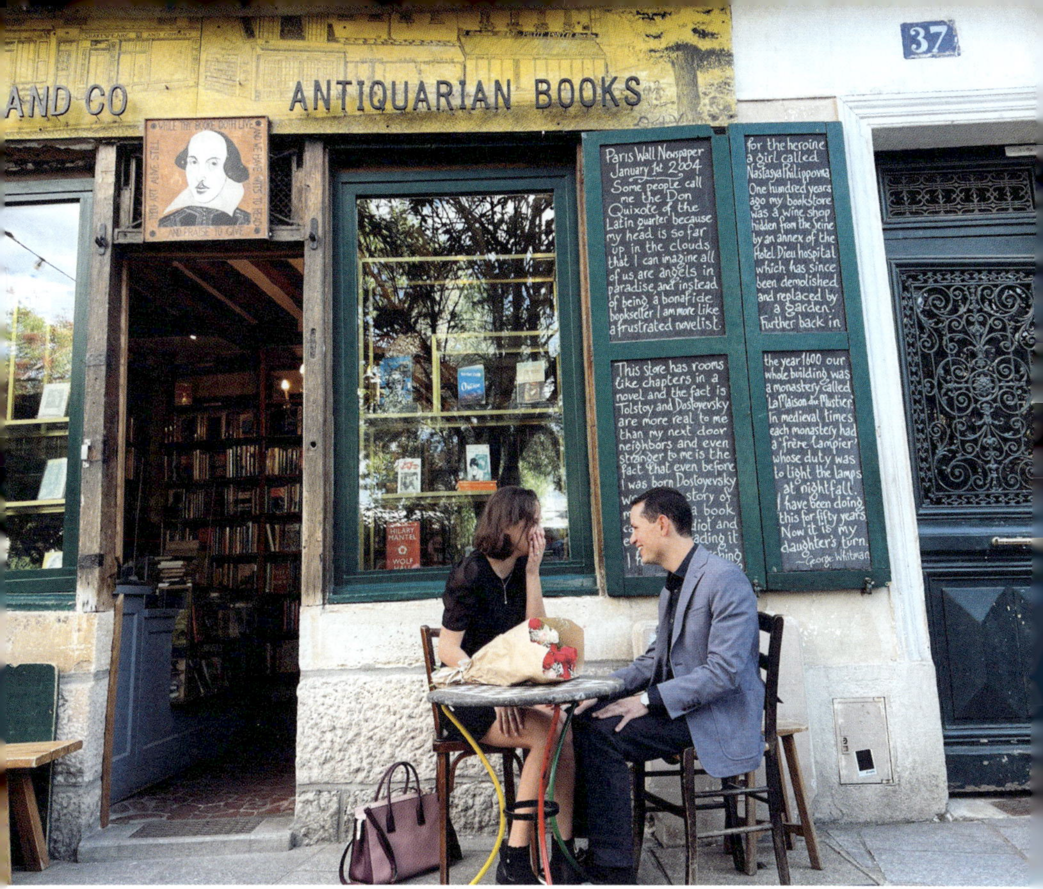

EMILY AND SAMUEL

Engaged: May 21, 2022 | Shakespeare and Company (Paris, France)

CITY OF LOVE: "We were two huge book nerds who bonded over Harry Potter," Emily said, describing how she first met Samuel in middle school in Bethesda, Maryland. In fact, one of his first gifts to her was a British edition of J. K. Rowling's debut novel, *Harry Potter and the Philosopher's Stone*.

Although they had been dating since high school, Samuel wasn't ready to propose until he was almost finished with graduate school. And he decided to do it in Paris, the city of love and romance. At the time, Samuel was a doctoral candidate in art history at Princeton University, and Emily was a children's book editor at Random House Children's Books.

The hardest part, Emily learned afterwards, was for Samuel to find a way to document the proposal, which he knew that she would want.

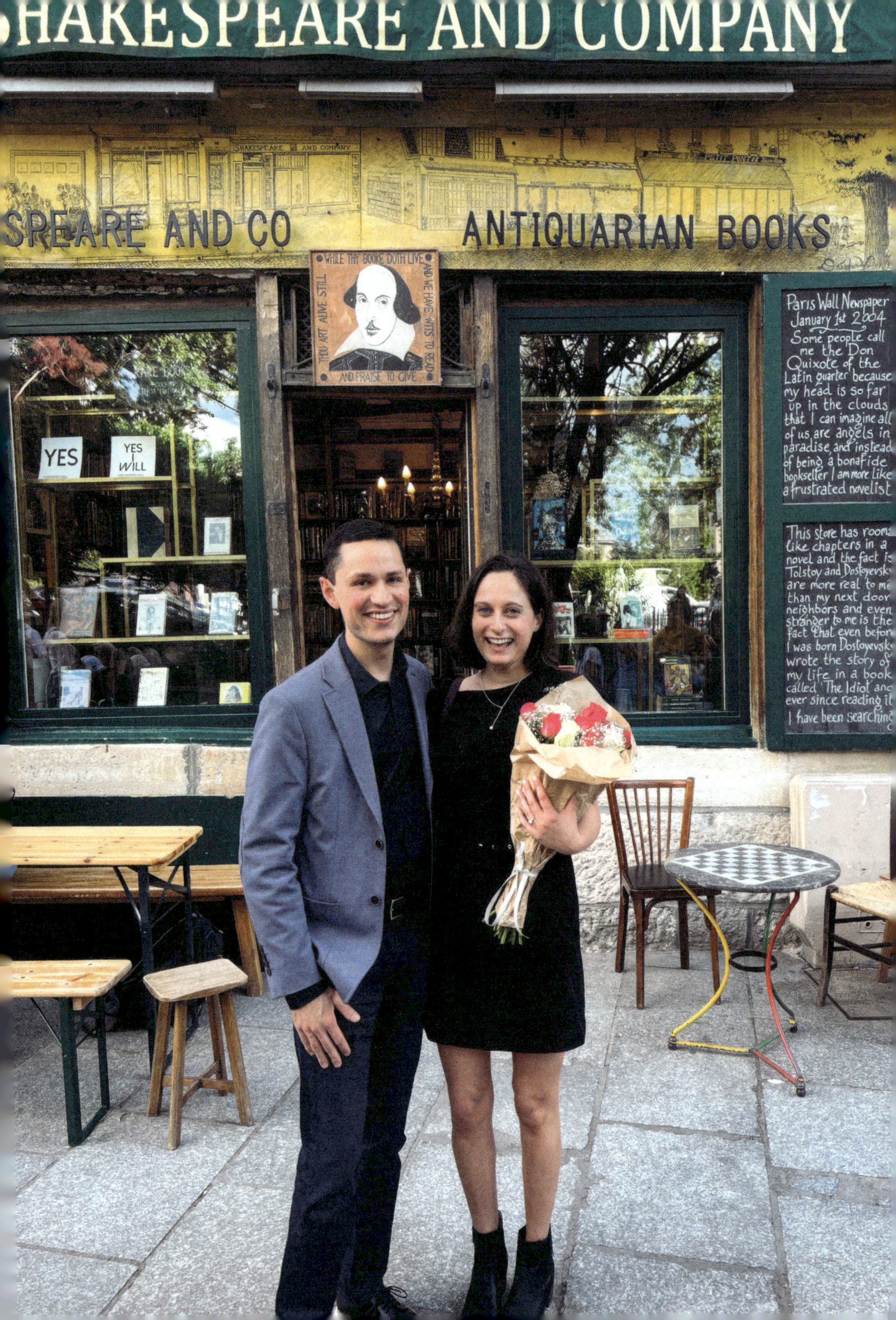

HAKESPEARE AND COMPANY
SPEARE AND CO
ANTIQUARIAN BOOKS
WHILE THY BOOKE DOTH LIVE AND WE HAVE WITS TO READ AND PRAISE TO GIVE THOU ART ALIVE STILL
YES
YES I WILL
Paris Wall Newspaper January 1st 2004 Some people call me the Don Quixote of the Latin quarter because my head is so far up in the clouds that I can imagine all of us are angels in paradise, and instead of being a bonafide bookseller I am more like a frustrated novelist
This store has room like chapters in a novel and the fact is Tolstoy and Dostoyevsk are more real to m than my next door neighbors and even stranger to me is the fact that even befor I was born Dostoyevsk wrote the story of my life in a book called 'The Idiot' and ever since reading it I have been searching

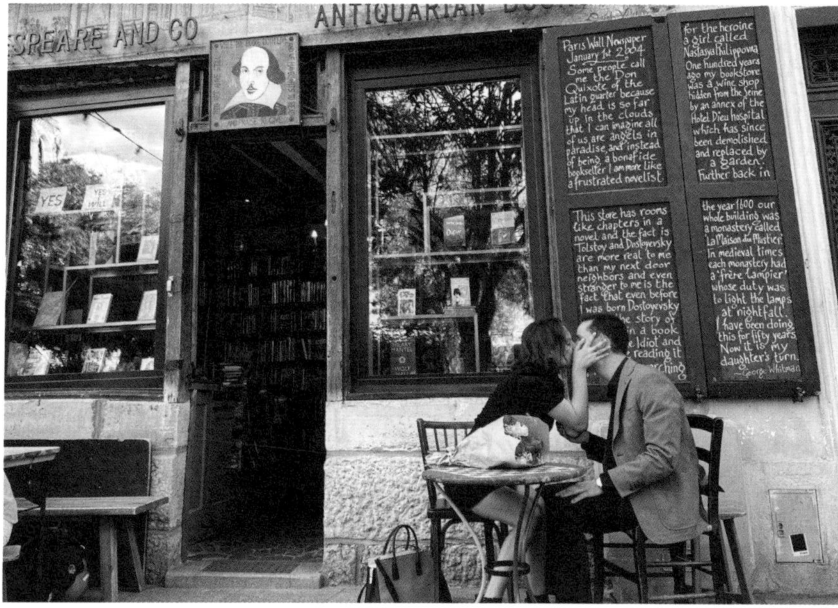

"Otherwise, I wouldn't have believed it," she said. Samuel's best friend, who later served as the best man at their wedding, volunteered his girlfriend's family. They would be traveling to Paris at the same time and could take photos and bring flowers for Samuel to give to Emily when she said "Yes." His parents had given him a family ring.

One thing that Samuel hadn't prepared for was their flight's late arrival, as they'd been delayed by more than four hours. Despite the extra-long travel time and jet lag, Samuel pressed Emily to join him on a walk to the famous English-language bookstore Shakespeare and Company. It's the namesake of the bookstore founded in 1919 by Sylvia Beach, which first published James Joyce's *Ulysses*. Emily readily agreed.

But there was a long line of people waiting to get in, so they spent some time browsing in the bookstore's antiquarian section next door, which had no line. When they were leaving, Samuel dropped to one knee on the bookstore's steps. Emily said that she was completely surprised by the proposal and in the moment, she wasn't aware of anyone else but them. Afterwards, she heard the applause from the waiting line.

The bookstore was "a perfect backdrop," Emily said. "I'm never happier than when I'm in a bookstore."

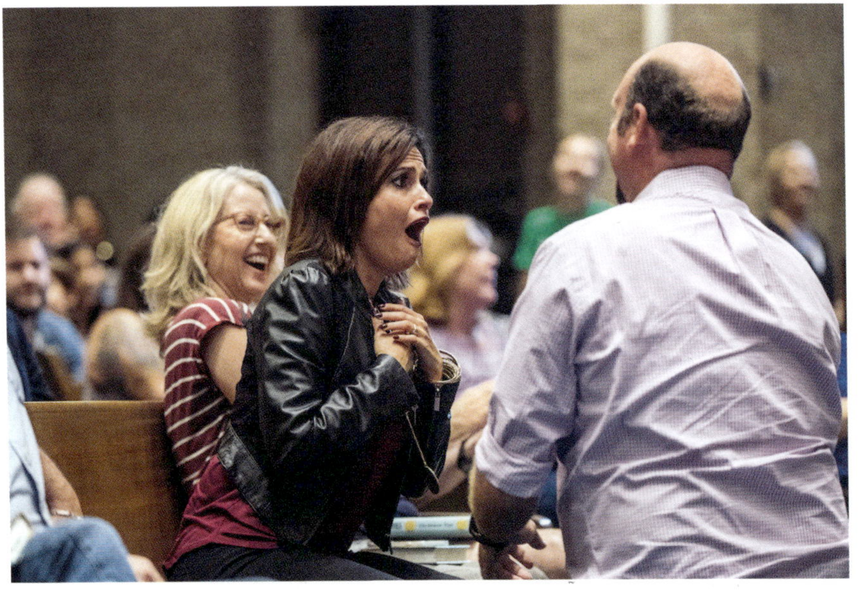

NIKKI AND RYAN

Engaged: November 4, 2017 **| Texas Book Festival (Austin, Texas)**

Q&A: Some people like to go big to show how much love they feel, and they propose via a billboard or movie theater screen. But since Nikki loves books, Ryan decided that the best way to express his love was by proposing at one of the country's largest book festivals, which draws fifty thousand attendees.

But even then, Ryan wanted to do more. So he enlisted the help of Academy Award-winning actor and author Tom Hanks, who was appearing at the festival to promote his short story collection, *Uncommon Type: Some Stories.*

As reported by ABC News, towards the end of his appearance Hanks announced that he was tired of answering questions and wanted to ask one of his own. Then he pulled out a piece of paper and asked, on behalf of Ryan, if Nikki would marry him.

TV cameras caught Nikki bursting into happy tears. Then, the couple joined Hanks on-stage, where Ryan got down on one knee. And he placed a ring on Nikki's finger. The proposal ended with Hanks putting his arm around the couple as if to give them his blessing.

He blessed the union in more ways than one. When Tom Hanks is involved, a book festival proposal can be very big indeed. It played on repeat on every TV news station, on social media, and in newspapers and magazines. And it's still one of the most memorable events to have taken place at the Texas Book Festival.

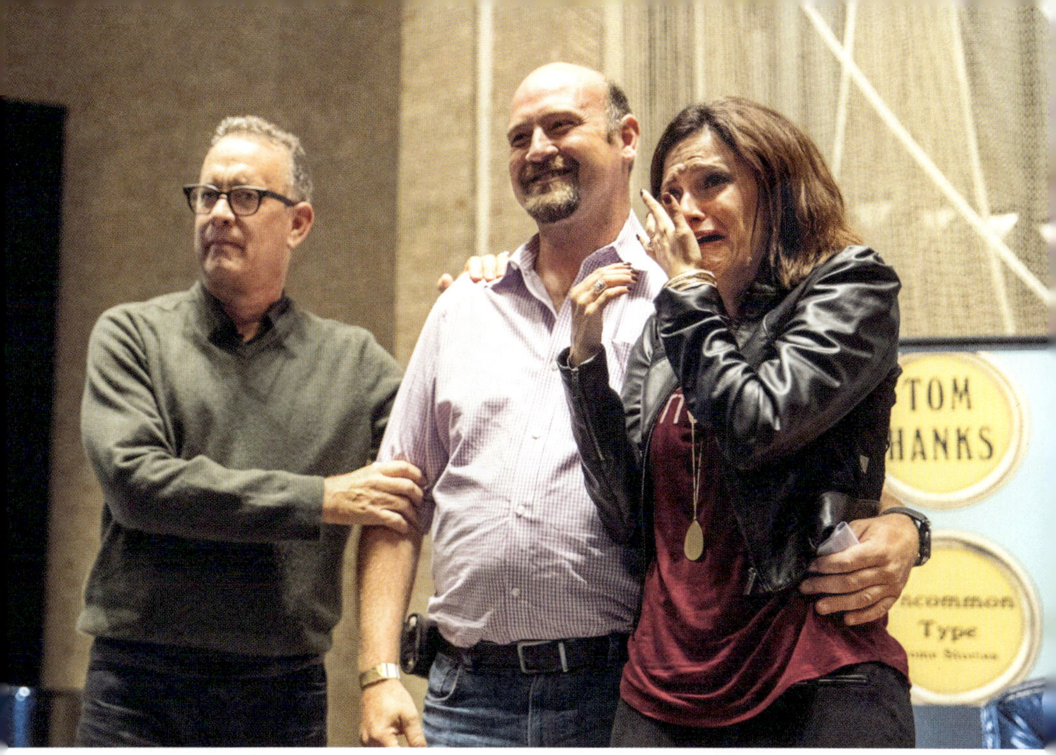
TOM
HANKS
Type

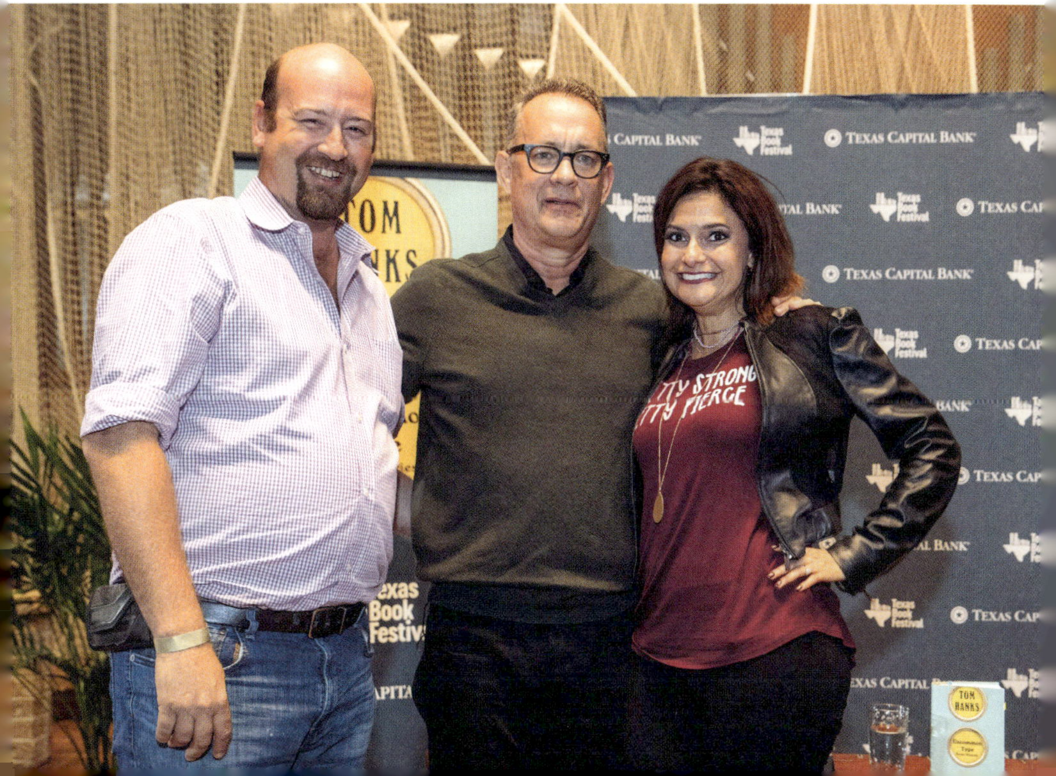
TEXAS CAPITAL BANK
Texas Book Festival
TOM
HANKS

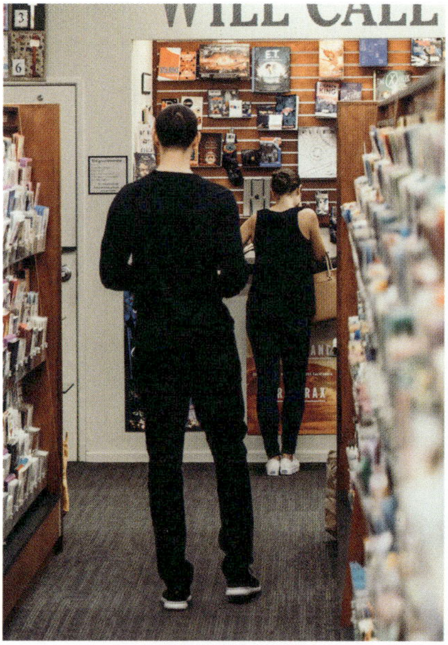
WILL CALL

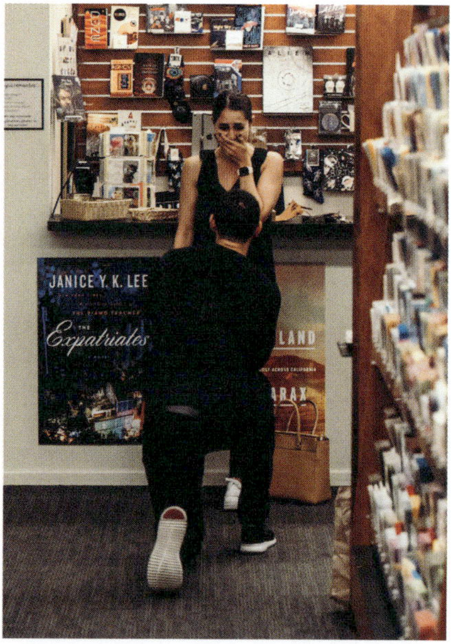
JANICE Y. K. LEE
The Expatriates

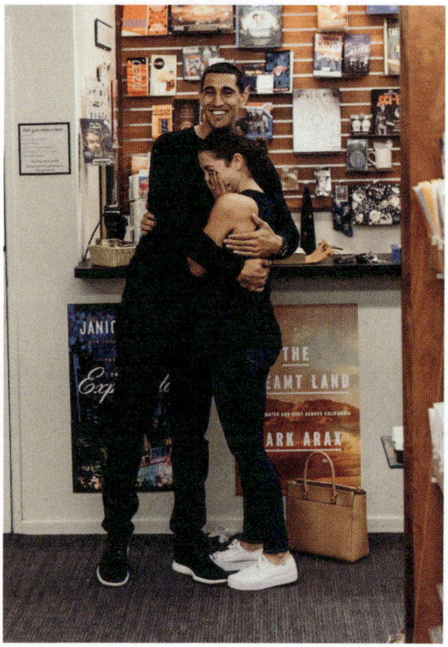

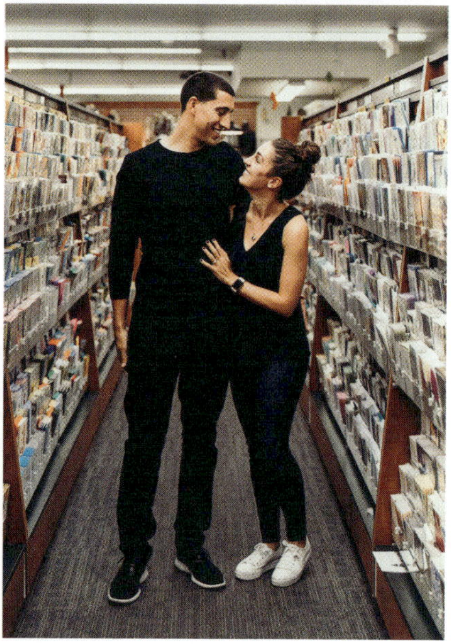

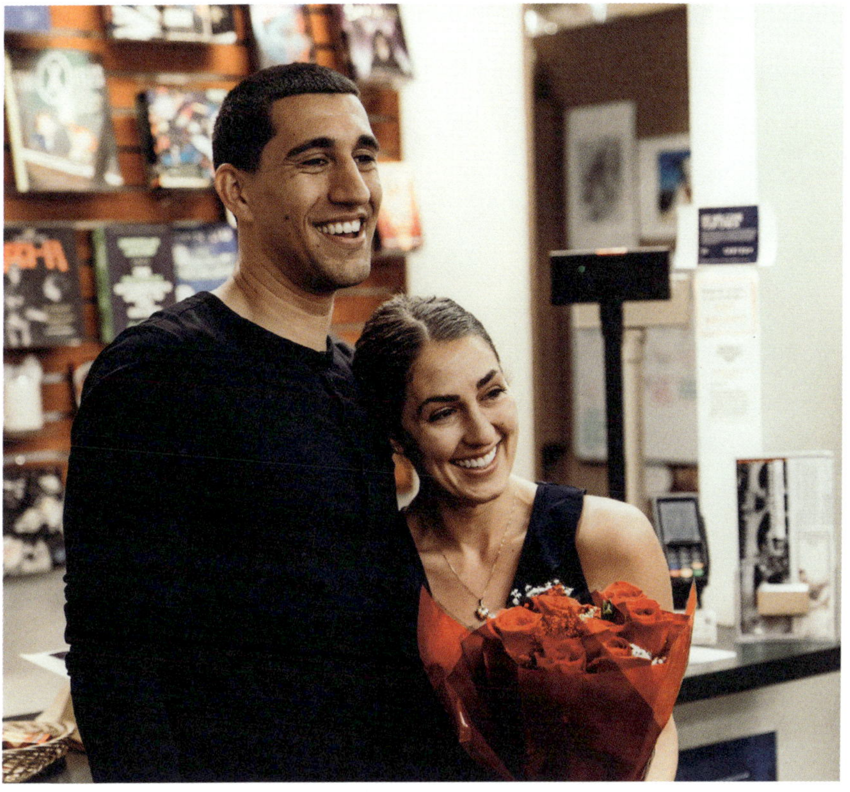

DAMAN AND JENA

Engaged: September 4, 2019 | Vroman's Bookstore (Pasadena, California)

SURPRISE!: Though Daman had never been to Jena's favorite store, Vroman's, he knew how important it was to her and that it was the very place to get engaged. To make sure that her family would be able to celebrate with them, he settled on the same date as an eighty-eighth birthday dinner that had been planned for her grandfather. But to keep it a surprise, he told Jena that he couldn't attend the dinner; he'd be in Las Vegas.

It may take a village to raise a child, but Daman found that it takes an entire family, plus several friends, to create the ultimate bookstore surprise proposal. He enlisted

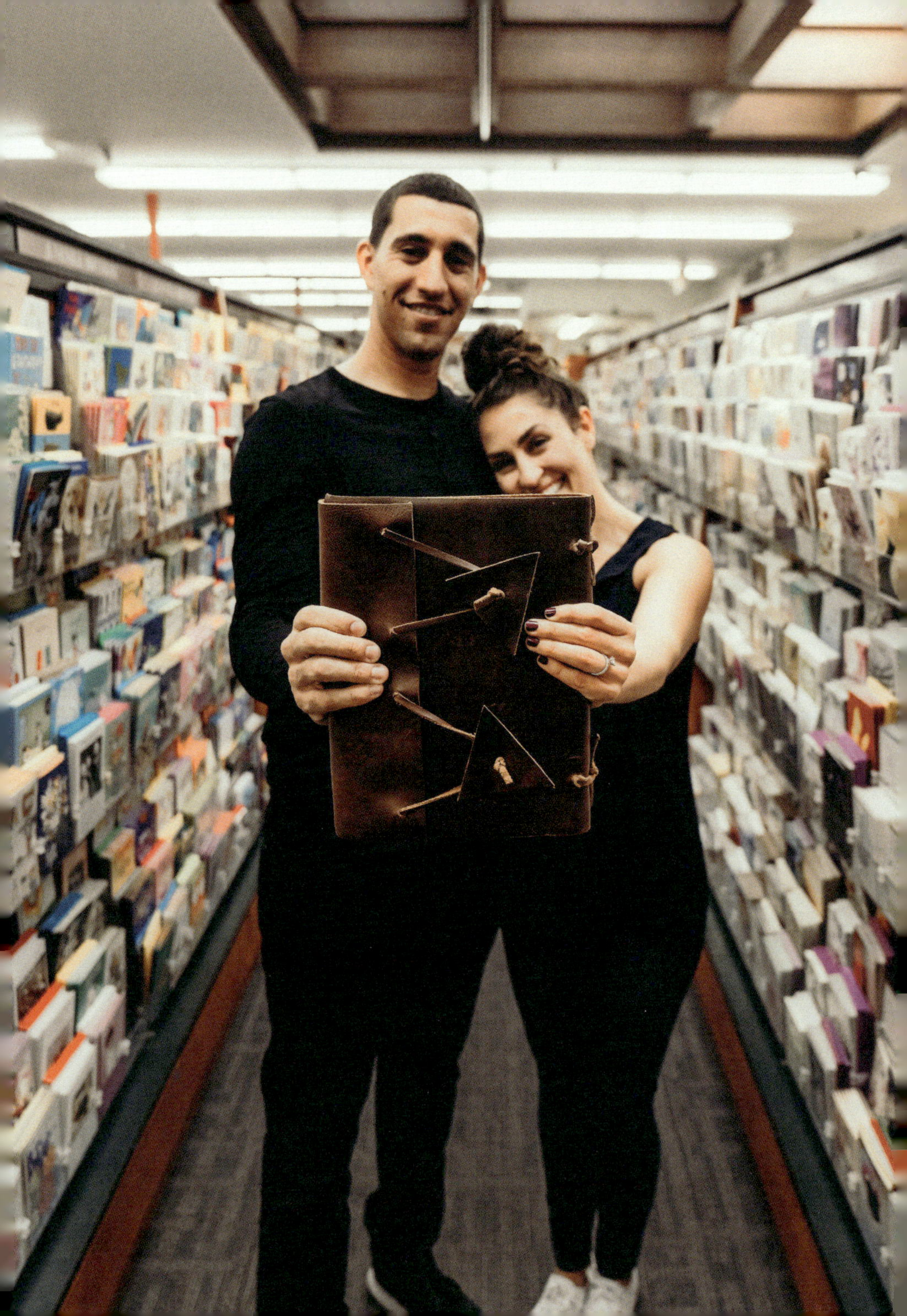

Jena's mother and aunt, children's book author and illustrator Marla Frazee, to get Vroman's permission. And he asked the family to write engagement wishes to Jena in an oversized leather-covered blank book that he had brought back from China years earlier and had been saving for when he got engaged, someday.

Daman found that it takes an entire family, plus several friends, to create the ultimate bookstore surprise proposal.

Jena's dad got her to the bookstore on the planned afternoon by texting her to ask if she would stop by Vroman's after work and pick up a book for her grandfather's birthday. It would be at the "Will Call" desk. It was, in fact, Daman's book, the one the family had signed.

The bookstore staff was in on the surprise engagement, too. When Jena arrived at "Will Call," the person behind the desk handed the book to her and opened it to the page that Daman had signed. The bookseller asked Jena to read it and make sure she was picking up the right book.

But Jena was having trouble focusing on Daman's note, which ended with the words "Turn around." She had no idea that he was in Pasadena, much less standing directly behind her. Despite the clearly written instruction, the bookseller at the desk had to remind Jena several times to look behind her.

"I was shocked," Jena said. "Everything was so perfect and well thought out. My best friend started taking pictures, and Daman's best friend handed me flowers."

As for Vroman's, it's still Jena's favorite store. "I try not to buy books anywhere else."

WEDDINGS *and* RECEPTIONS

BREONNA

Wedding: August 31, 2014 | Brazos Bookstore (Houston, Texas)

HERE COMES THE BRIDE: When Breonna told her fiancé that instead of engagement photos she wanted to have a bridal portrait taken at Brazos, he readily agreed. "You're in there all the time. Go for it." And go for it she did.

A strong tradition in the south, where Breonna lives, bridal portrait sessions give brides a chance to try out their wedding look—makeup, hair, and dress—ahead of the actual ceremony. Because there's no pressure, brides-to-be often look more relaxed than on their wedding day.

While some women choose garden venues or public parks, Breonna wanted to be in her happy place, surrounded by books. "I've always been into reading. It's always been my jam," she said. As Brazos was an atypical choice for bridal photos, this was a first for the bookstore, which only asked that Breonna come at a slow time on a weekday afternoon.

After Breonna transformed from a working woman into a bride by putting on her gorgeous wedding dress in the store bathroom, the staff helped her and photographer Emily Ross get the best shots with the best natural light by rearranging the display cases. Forty-five minutes later the two women emerged with a sequence of photos that captured Breonna's warm personality, her beautiful smile, and the chucks that she wore underneath her dress. For the actual wedding, Breonna chose ballet flats. She didn't want to trip.

As a book lover, Breonna has a large, and growing, home library. "The more digitized stuff gets, the more I collect paper," she said.

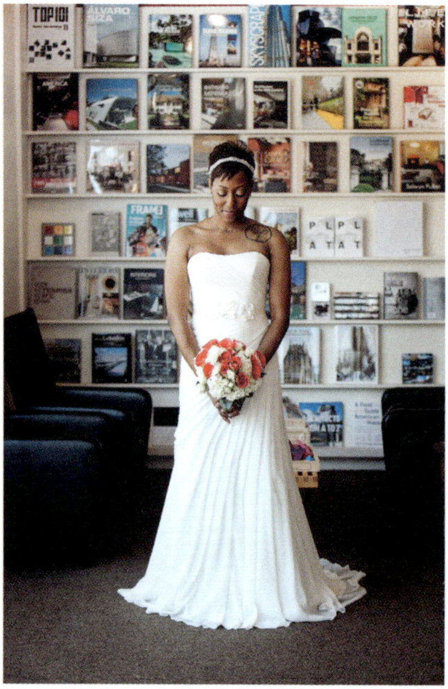

During Covid, she tried writing her own books and self-published two of them. Although she likes to read widely, she prefers writing romance, at least for now.

Breonna passed on her love of reading to her now teenaged daughter. "We do buddy reads," she said. "We buy books two at a time." Her daughter, who gets the final choice, gravitates to newly published books, especially graphic novels. It's too soon to know if she also inherited the writing gene, or if she'll also choose bookstore bridal photos to celebrate her big day.

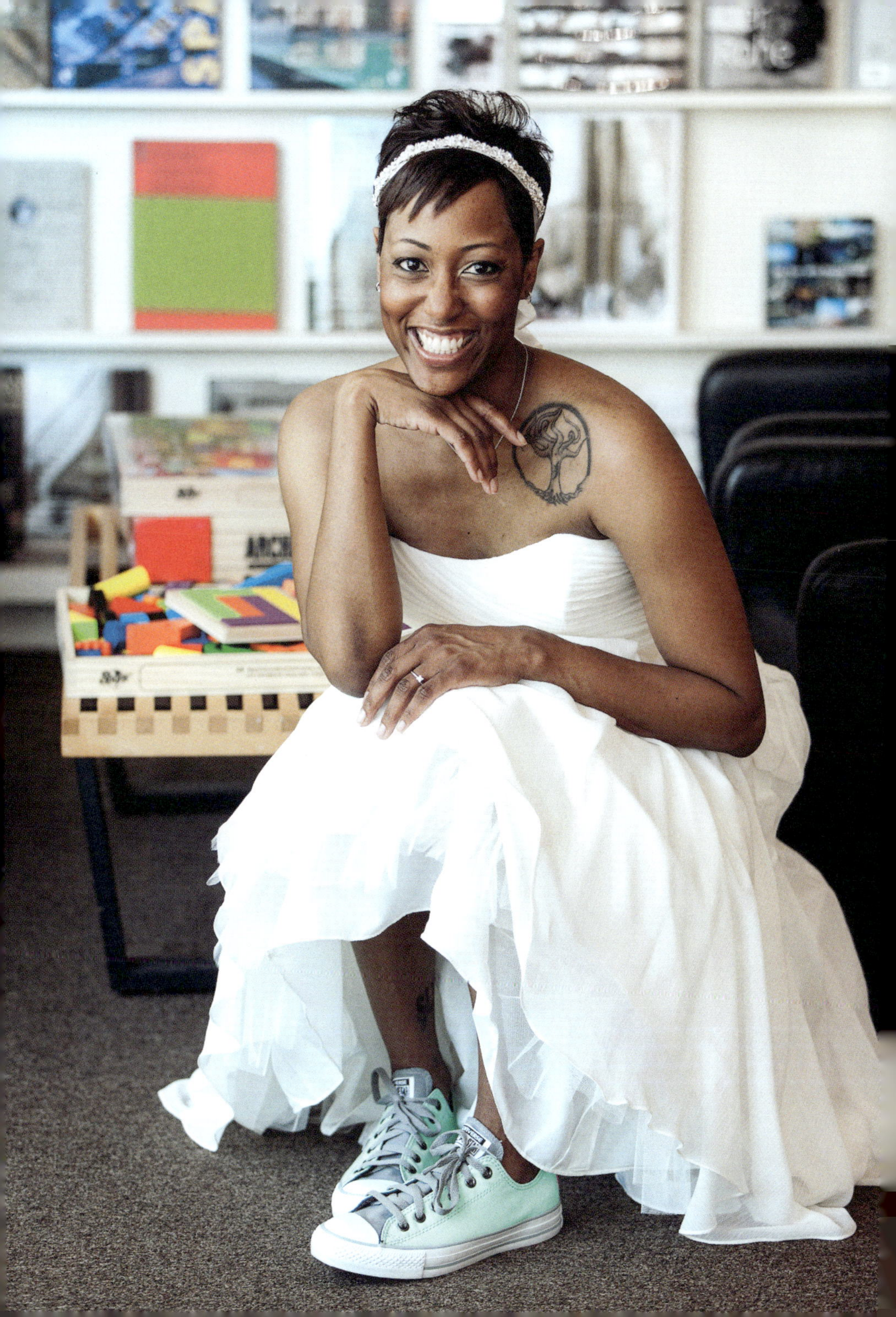

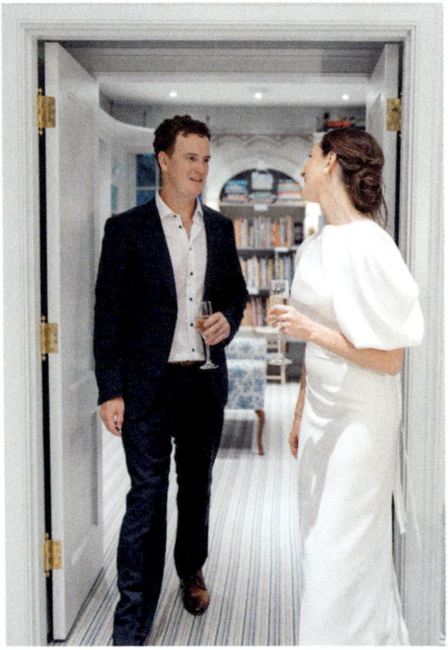

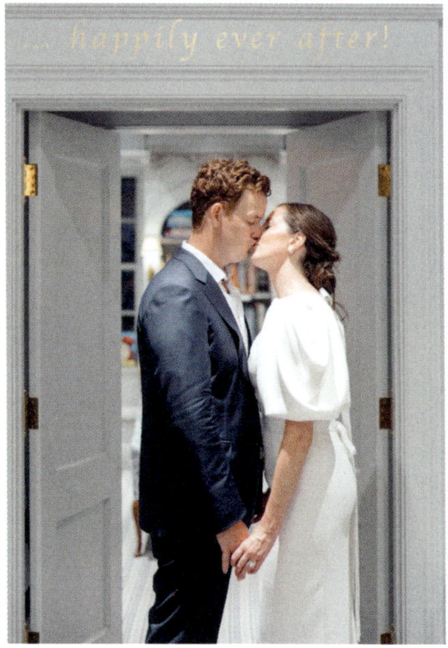

CAITRIN AND KEITH

Wedding: September 7, 2023 | Beacon Hill Books & Cafe (Boston, Massachusetts)

MAKING MEMORIES: Although Caitrin and Keith live in Charleston, South Carolina, they wanted a small church wedding in Boston near her family, as well as a very special place to hold their reception dinner. The couple knew that they had found exactly what they wanted when they saw a proposal photo taken at Beacon Hill Books & Cafe, a five-story renovated townhouse that opened on September 30, 2022, in the historic Beacon Hill neighborhood of Boston.

For Caitrin, who works in book publishing, the elegant bookstore offered the kind of unique experience, surrounded by books, that she wanted for her wedding day. To make the event more special, she and Keith decided not to tell their guests the name of the venue in advance and to make it a surprise.

The store was still relatively new. Most guests had no idea where they were headed as Keith and Caitrin led the wedding party on a mile-and-a-half walk in 90-degree heat from their hotel near the Boston Public Garden to the bookstore.

The couple had rented the entire space to celebrate their big day. The reception was

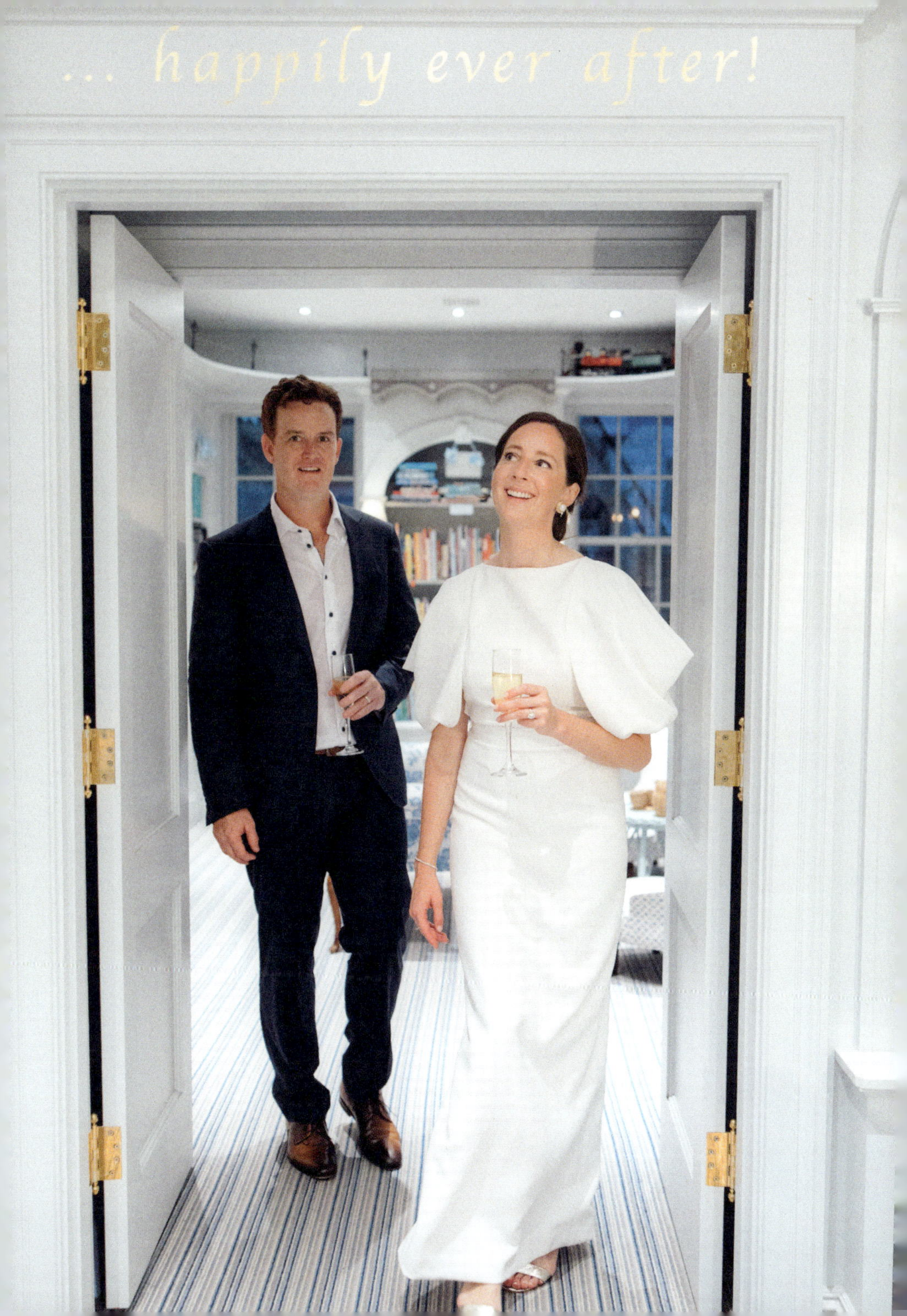
... happily ever after!

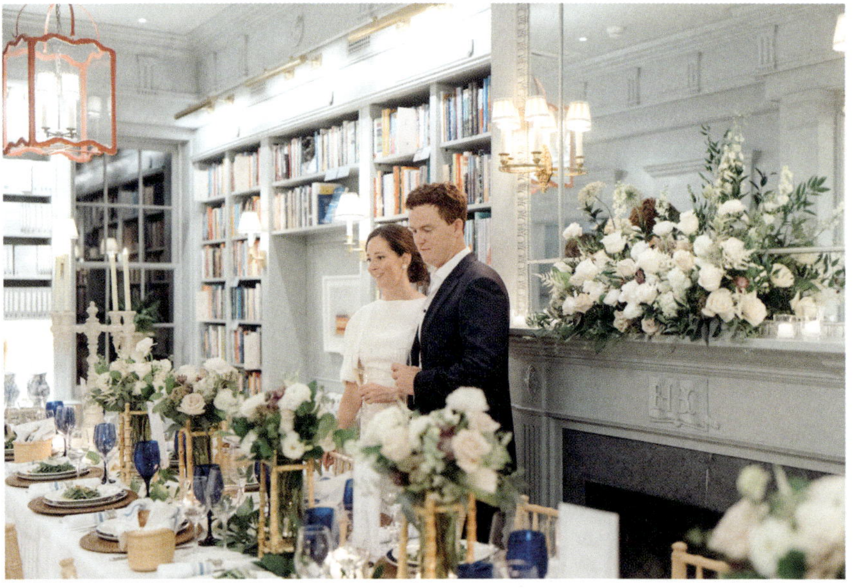

held in the second-floor fiction room at a long wooden table that had been cleared of new releases for the event. The children in the group quickly found their way one floor up to the space devoted to children's books.

Photographer Stephanie Berenson took many candid shots of the newlyweds and their guests. "My philosophy is to transport a person back to their wedding day. I take that as a big honor. I love to be able to create art and memories for generations," she said.

It was on the third floor of the bookstore in the children's area where Stephanie captured one of the most romantic moments of Caitrin and Keith's big day, a kiss in the doorway that was marked with gold lettering above it: ". . . happily ever after!"

There's a reason that this is the way many of the best stories end.

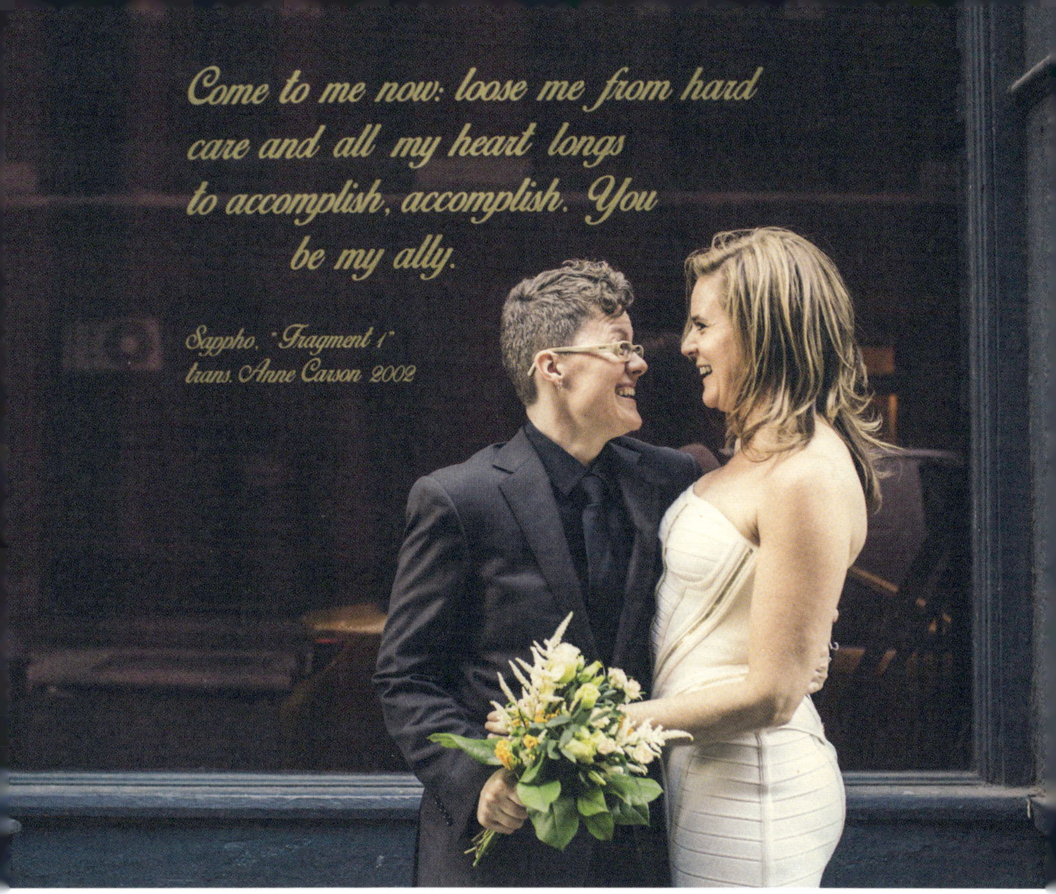

ANNA AND JILL

Wedding: August 20, 2015 | Housing Works Bookstore (New York, New York)

FLAWLESS WEDDING: Artists and academicians Jill and Anna chose New York City's Housing Works Bookstore for their big day. In part, no doubt, they were drawn to the storybook possibilities of one of New York City's most beautiful venues with its spiral staircases, mahogany balconies, and many volumes of books.

But the good that Housing Works does not only contributes to its numerous five-star ratings on wedding sites like The Knot and Wedding Wire but likely also appealed to Anna and Jill for their queer wedding. This nonprofit bookstore donates all the proceeds from weddings and other events held there to benefit unhoused people living with HIV/AIDS.

The couple's wedding took place less than two months after the US Supreme Court's

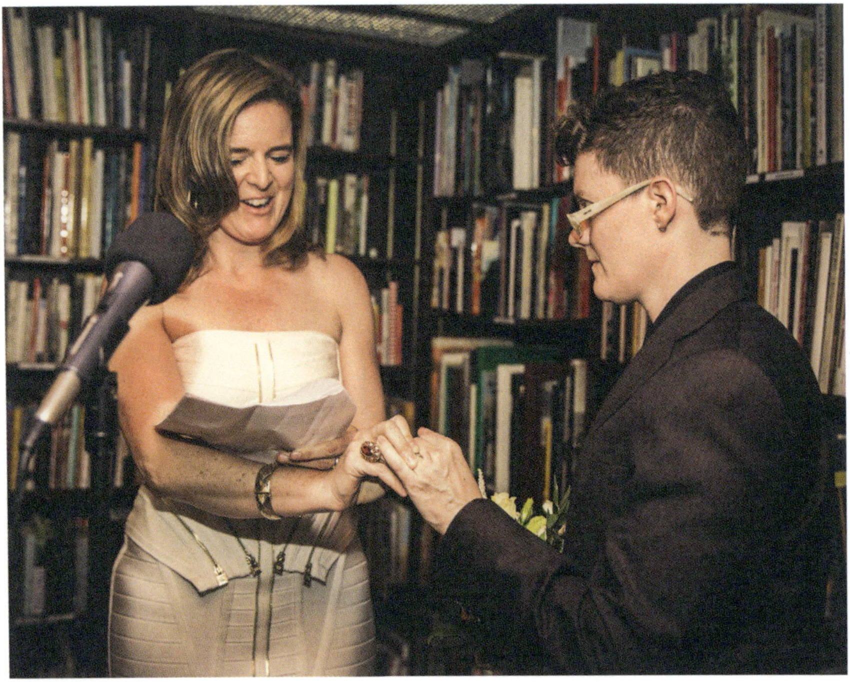

historic 5–4 decision in *Obergefell v. Hodges*, which gives same-sex couples the same legal right to marry as opposite-sex couples. Fittingly, Anna and Jill were joined in matrimony by "New York City Queer Icon" Flawless Sabrina, aka Jack Doroshow.

"No union is more profound than marriage, for it embodies the highest ideals of love, fidelity, devotion, sacrifice, and family," reads the court's majority opinion. "In forming a marital union, two people become something greater than they once were."

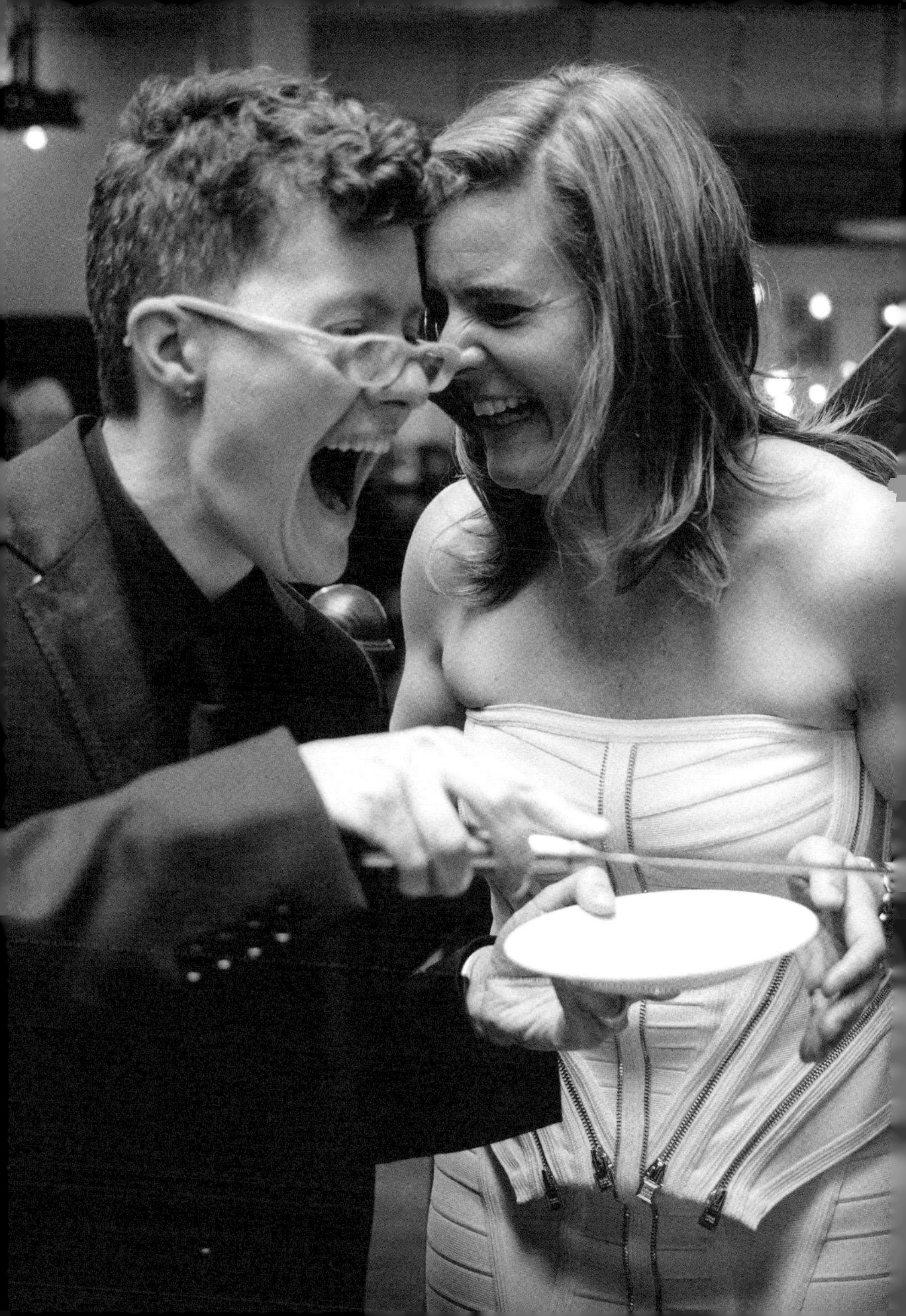

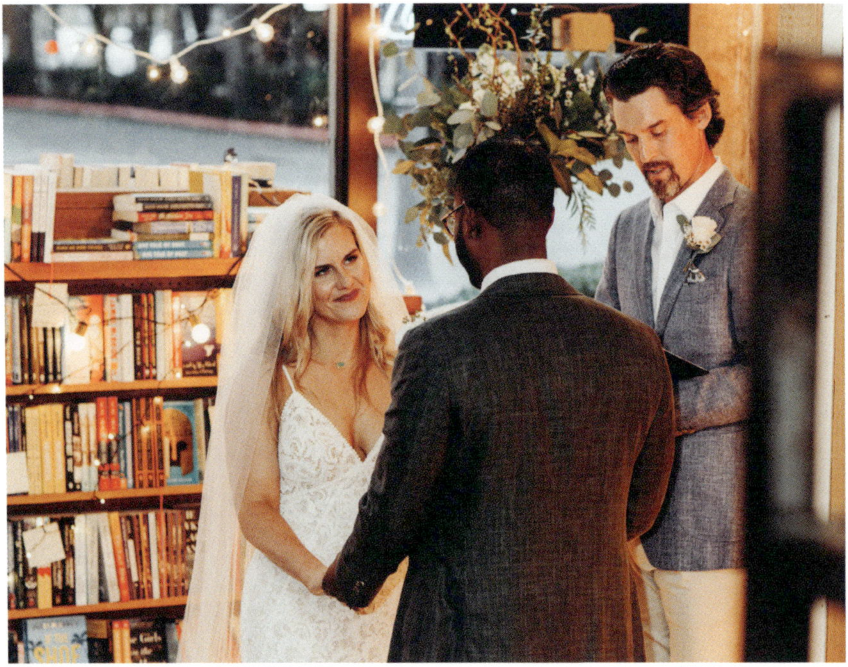

RYAN AND SARAH

Wedding: January 24, 2022 | Island Books (Mercer Island, Washington)

COVID PIVOT: When Oscar Wilde wrote, "To expect the unexpected shows a thoroughly modern intellect," he wasn't thinking about planning a wedding during the Covid pandemic. But the unexpected is exactly what Sarah and Ryan faced just two weeks before their destination wedding in Los Cabos, Mexico.

The couple was forced to ditch their plans and look closer to home for a venue in the Seattle area after Sarah's father, a physician, called to warn them about the increasing number of Covid cases due to the Omicron variant. Even though everyone on the guest list was vaccinated and boosted, if they were to get sick, it might be hard to get back into the US.

After Sarah hung up the phone, she cried, took a shower, ate a chocolate chip cookie, then pulled herself together and wrote an Instagram post asking her friends for help finding a new wedding venue with very little

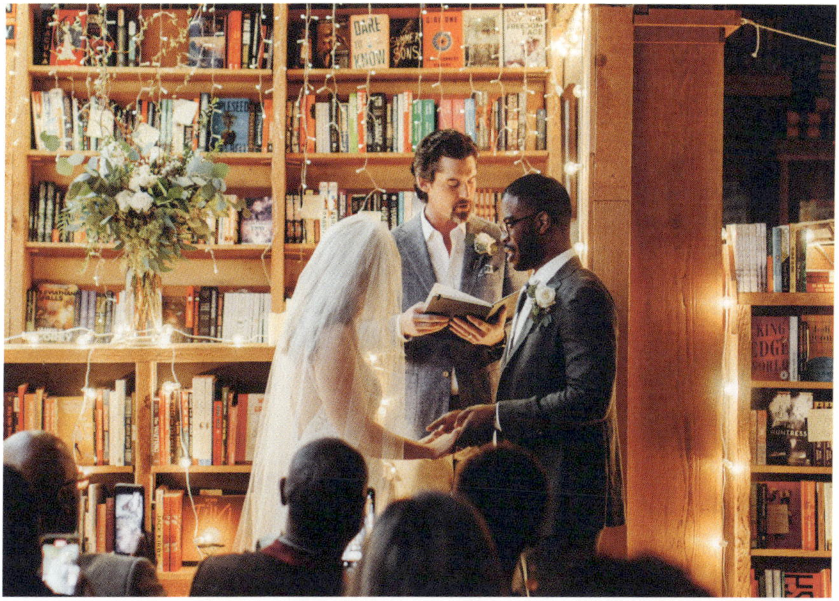
DARE TO KNOW
SUMMER SONS
HUNTRESS

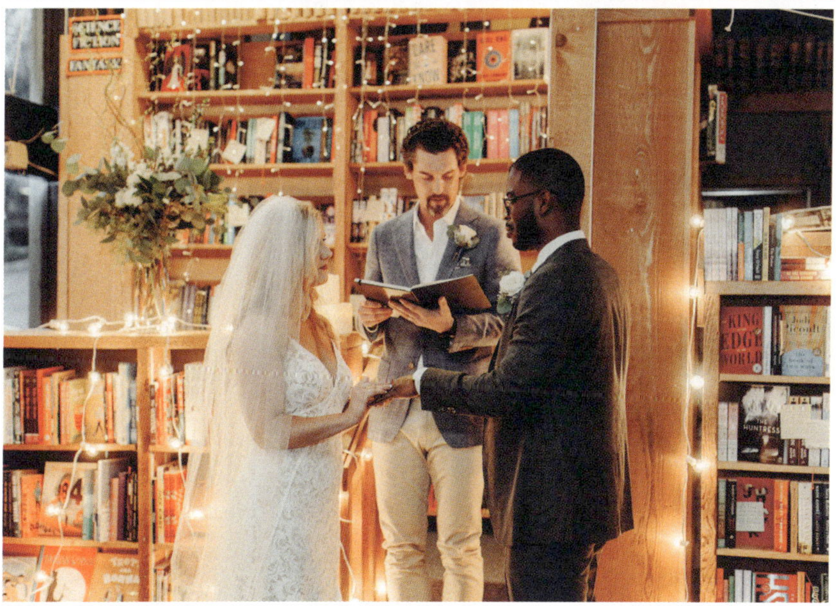
SCIENCE FICTION
FANTASY
HUNTRESS

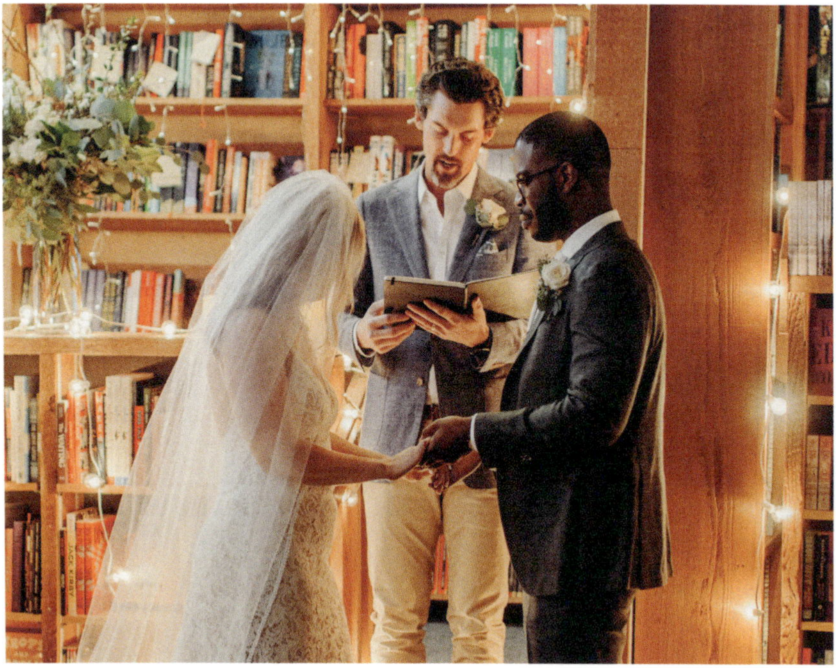

time. Laurie Raisys, owner of Island Books, responded immediately. She could host the wedding and fit all forty-five guests. It might be a little tight, but it would work. Sarah's family pitched in, too. Her sister got candles and twinkle lights to make the bookstore cozy, and her brother-in-law officiated. Those outside the Northwest rerouted their flights. And Ryan's grandmother joined them via Facetime.

Sarah and Ryan had no ties to Mexico, but Sarah had grown up at Island Books. And books and reading have been an important part of the couple's life together, so much so that they had many dates at the downtown Seattle Public Library and the Elliot Bay Book Company.

For Sarah, the wedding was "special and intimate," and neither she and Ryan nor their friends and family had ever been to a wedding in a bookstore before. Now Island Books is where Sarah and Ryan celebrate their anniversary. Since the birth of their son, they bring him to the store as well to see where his parents, who got engaged during Covid in July 2020, were married at the height of the pandemic.

"I got the wedding I didn't know I wanted," Sarah said. "Our Plan B wedding was a million times better than the wedding we had planned would have been."

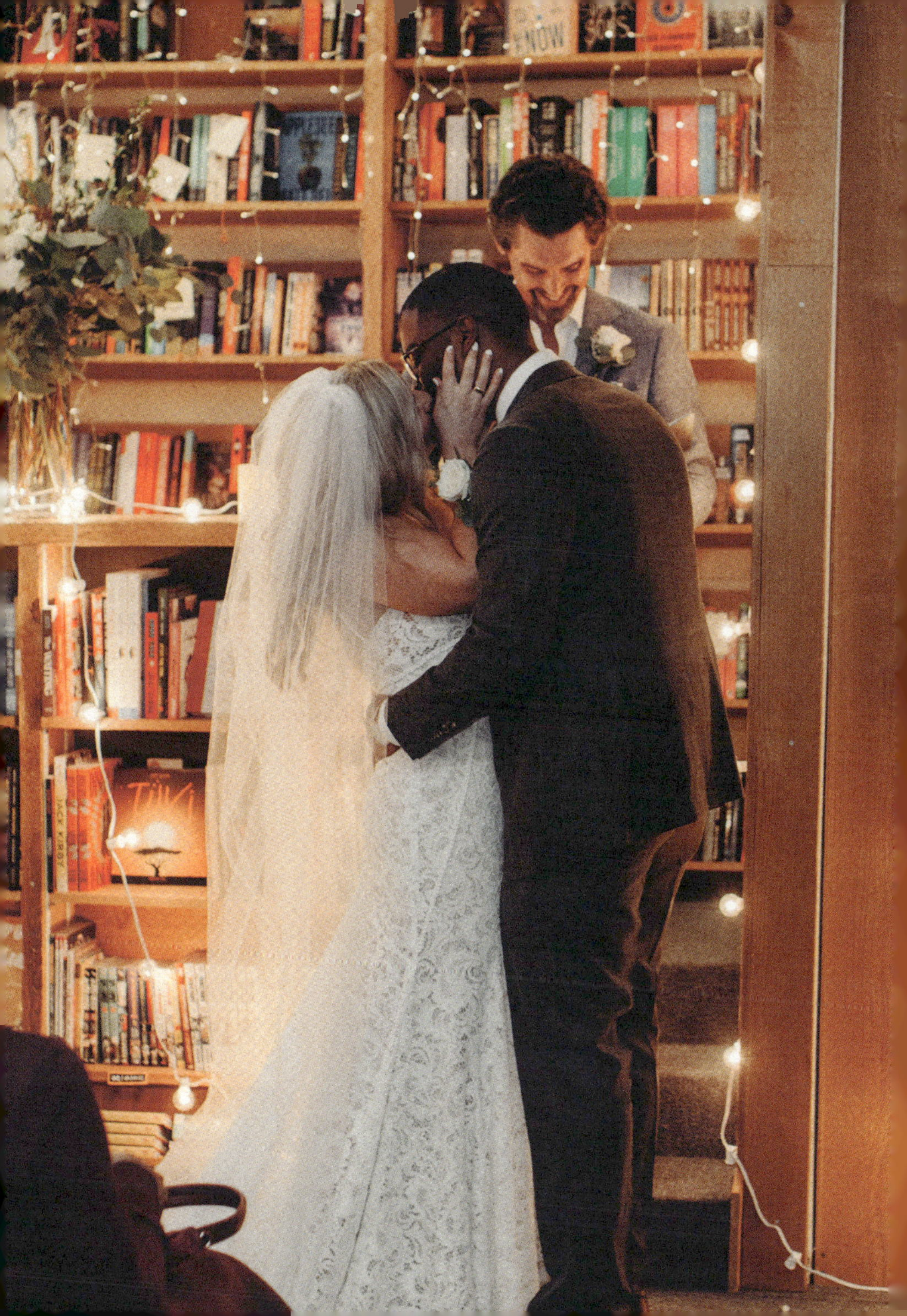
#NOW
JACK KIRBY

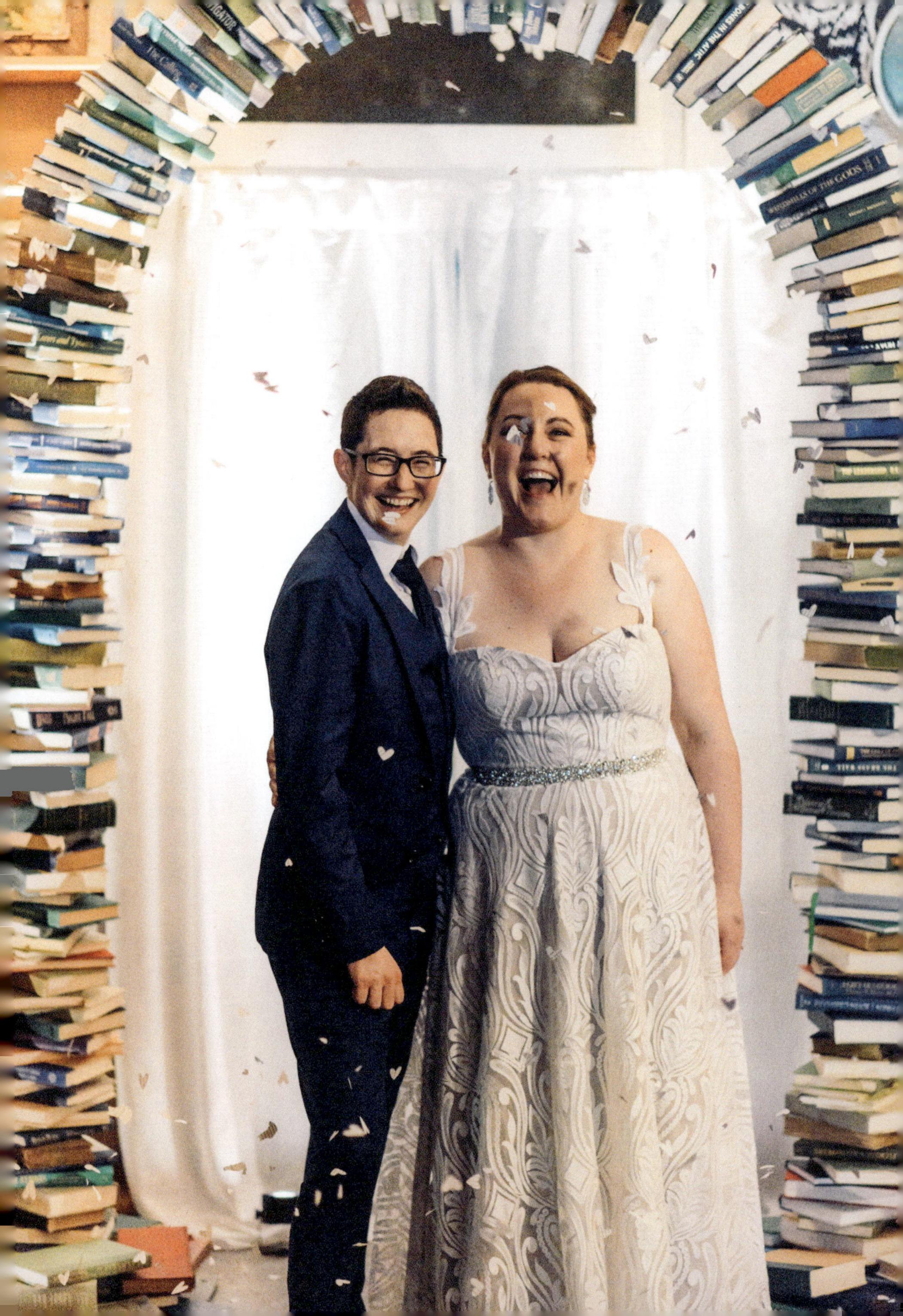

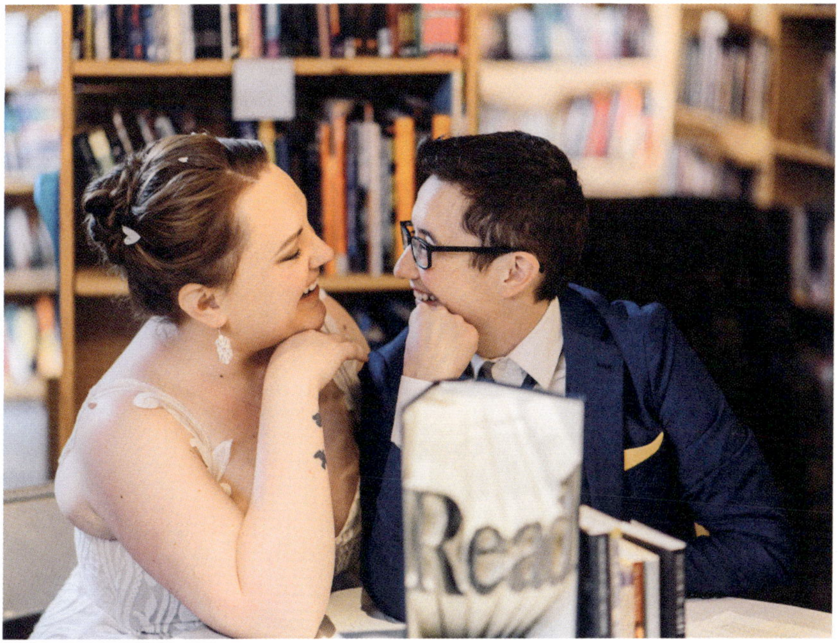

ERIN AND KIM

Married: July 23, 2022 | King's Books (Tacoma, Washington)

MUST LOVE BOOKS! A long-time bookseller, who is currently director of education at the American Booksellers Association, Kim couldn't imagine sharing a life with someone who didn't like to read. Fortunately, they found their perfect match on Tinder. A licensed mental health worker, Erin just might be even more of a voracious reader than Kim.

Kim's proposal was by the book, literally. They made a Lego book and added customized photos of Erin, their cats, and other meaningful moments in their life together. As for the wedding, the couple agreed that it had to be in a bookstore, where they would be surrounded by books, family, and friends.

Erin's only rule was that they couldn't hold the wedding at Third Place Books at Seward Park, which Kim managed at the time. She didn't want Kim to get behind the register and start working during the festivities. Instead, the pair chose a bookstore closer to Erin's family in the Olympia area: King's Books, which is known for its community events and annual letterpress festival.

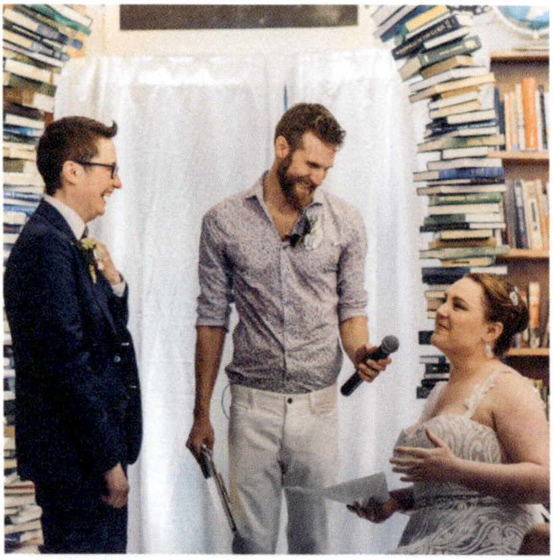

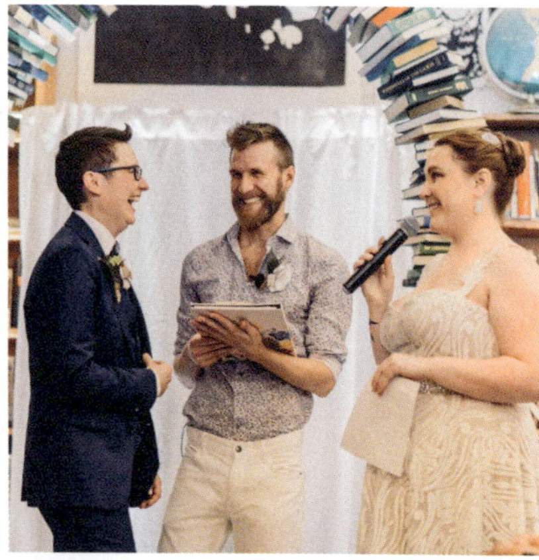

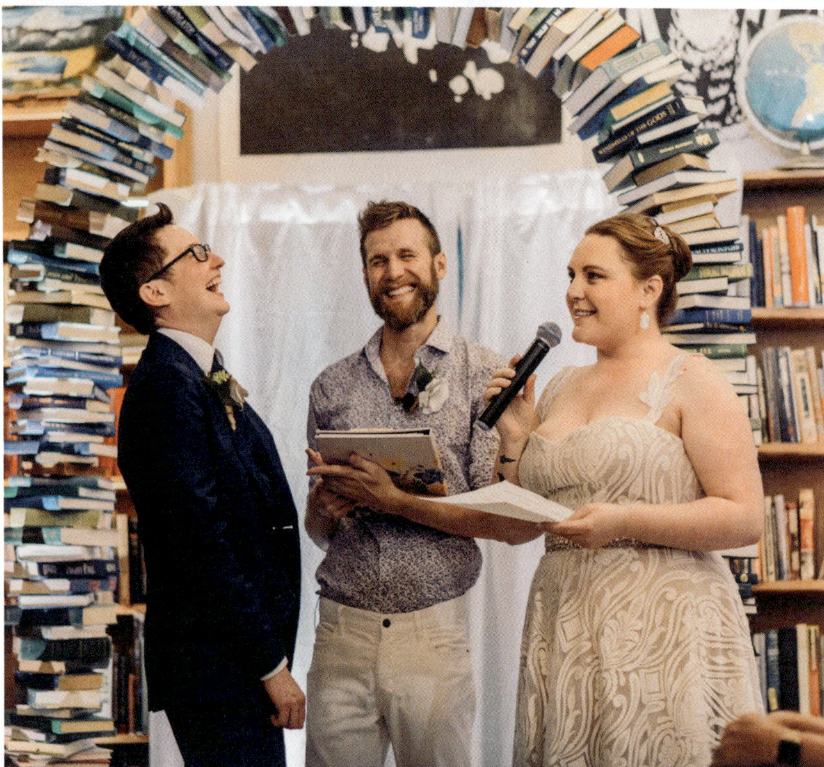

But Erin and Kim's decision to have a bookish wedding didn't stop there. The couple chose bookmarks for their save-the-date mailing to friends and family. And Kim tracked down a book arch that she had seen online, so that they could get married surrounded by even more books. The décor was also book inspired. Erin made decorations with their initials and with the word "love" by folding pages in books. The couple repurposed galleys (advance copies of forthcoming books that are sent to booksellers and reviewers) to make a book bouquet for Erin and to create confetti.

> *It was the perfect space. There was such a spirit of community.*

In the months leading up to the ceremony, their officiant asked them about their favorite authors. Then at the wedding he surprised them with quotations about love and the literary life by those very same writers, printed on small pieces of paper. He threw the quotes out to those who were gathered for the wedding. Then he called upon the recipients to read the quotes aloud as part of the ceremony.

Erin, Kim, and their friends and family had the store to themselves for the wedding. It was closed to customers, but continued to fulfill curbside orders. Guests could also purchase books. King's owner, sweet pea Flaherty, ordered multiple copies of the couples' favorite books and displayed them face out where store bestsellers are normally featured.

"It was the perfect space. There was such a spirit of community," Erin said of their decision to get married and hold their wedding reception at King's.

MATRIMONY MONDAYS

Facing, top: Peter and Tal were among the first to be married inside Pocket Books Shop.

bottom: Sarah and Ian were the very first couple to be married at the store.

SOON AFTER POCKET BOOKS SHOP, WHICH DESCRIBES ITSELF as "an eclectic feminist bookstore," opened on Independent Bookstore Day, April 30, 2022, in Lancaster, Pennsylvania, the owners decided to expand the shop's reach. The two-story new and used bookstore, in an old house with a wrap-around porch and parking lot, began renting out its space by the hour for small weddings on three bank holiday Mondays per year.

Matrimony Mondays, as the store calls the six back-to-back micro-wedding slots they offer, were particularly popular during Covid. "It's been really fun," said Jessica Callahan, who describes the bookstore marriages as a more personal alternative to courthouse weddings.

Callahan, who founded the bookstore with Austin Carter and Julie Ross, hadn't planned on holding weddings as part of the bookstore's events lineup. But she said, "We decided to really commit to the dream" of having a bookstore. They decided to try micro-weddings at the suggestion of their friend, Mary Aukers-Endres, an officiant with Journeys of the Heart, a nondenominational ministry.

The timing works well for the store, which holds the weddings either indoors or outside on the porch, with guests seated on the lawn. Couples rent the space for sixty-minute slots and are asked to arrive on the hour; the ceremony starts promptly ten minutes later. Callahan works with the couple in advance to help them plan how they want to spend their hour, which frequently includes cake cutting, photographs, and book browsing in addition to the ceremony.

Aukers-Endres officiates weddings for the bookstore. She honed her micro-wedding skills officiating for the City of Philadelphia's Parks & Recreation Department's Wedding Wednesdays, which are held outdoors in front of the LOVE sculpture in Love Park. At Pocket Books, local photographer Michelle Johnsen captures key moments for the couple. Both Johnsen's and Aukers-Endres's services are included as part of a flat fee for the wedding. Couples can also create a wedding registry on the store's website.

For a longer event, couples can rent the entire bookstore space after hours. Pocket Books will also coordinate decorations, catering, entertainment, and everything else that's needed. In addition to weddings, the store has been the location for half a dozen proposals . . . at no cost.

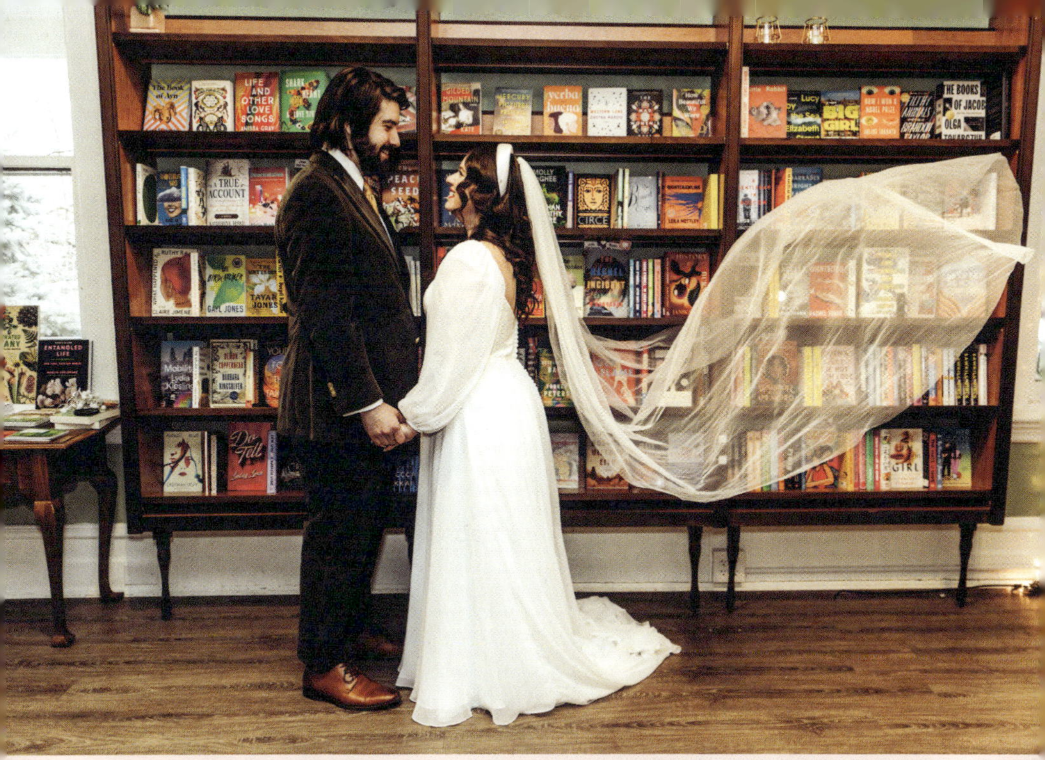
LIFE AND OTHER LOVE SONGS
yerba buena
A TRUE ACCOUNT
CIRCE
ENTANGLED LIFE
GAYL JONES
BARBARA KINGSOLVER
Do Tell
THE BOOKS OF JACOB
GIRL

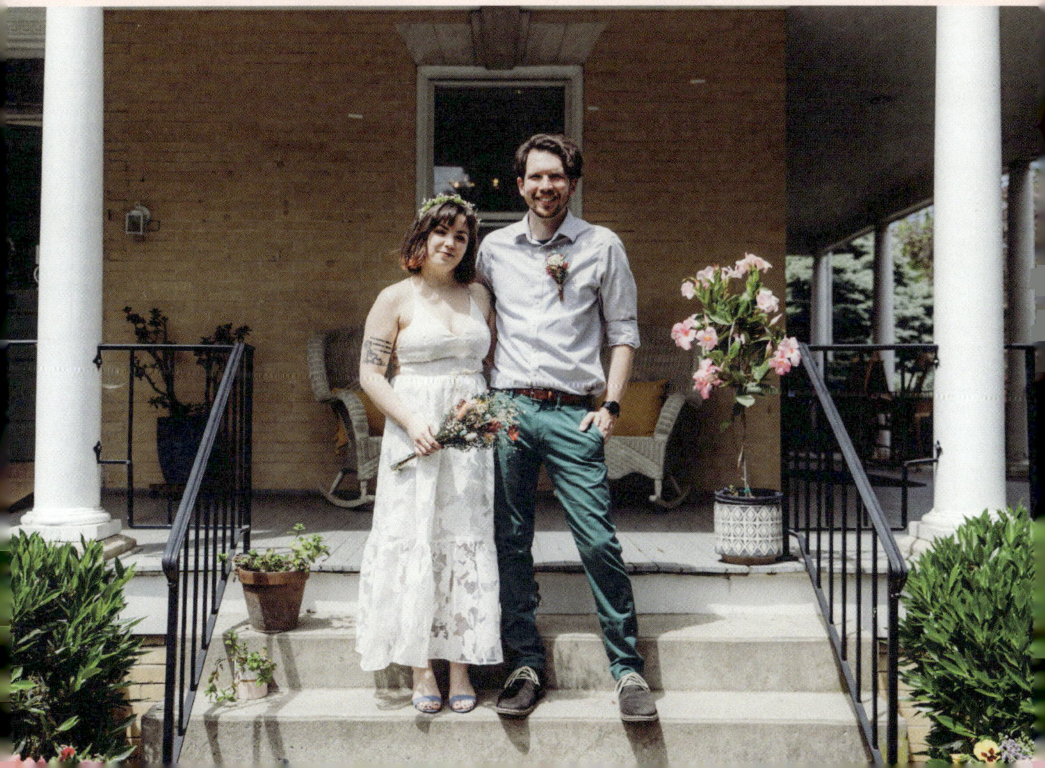

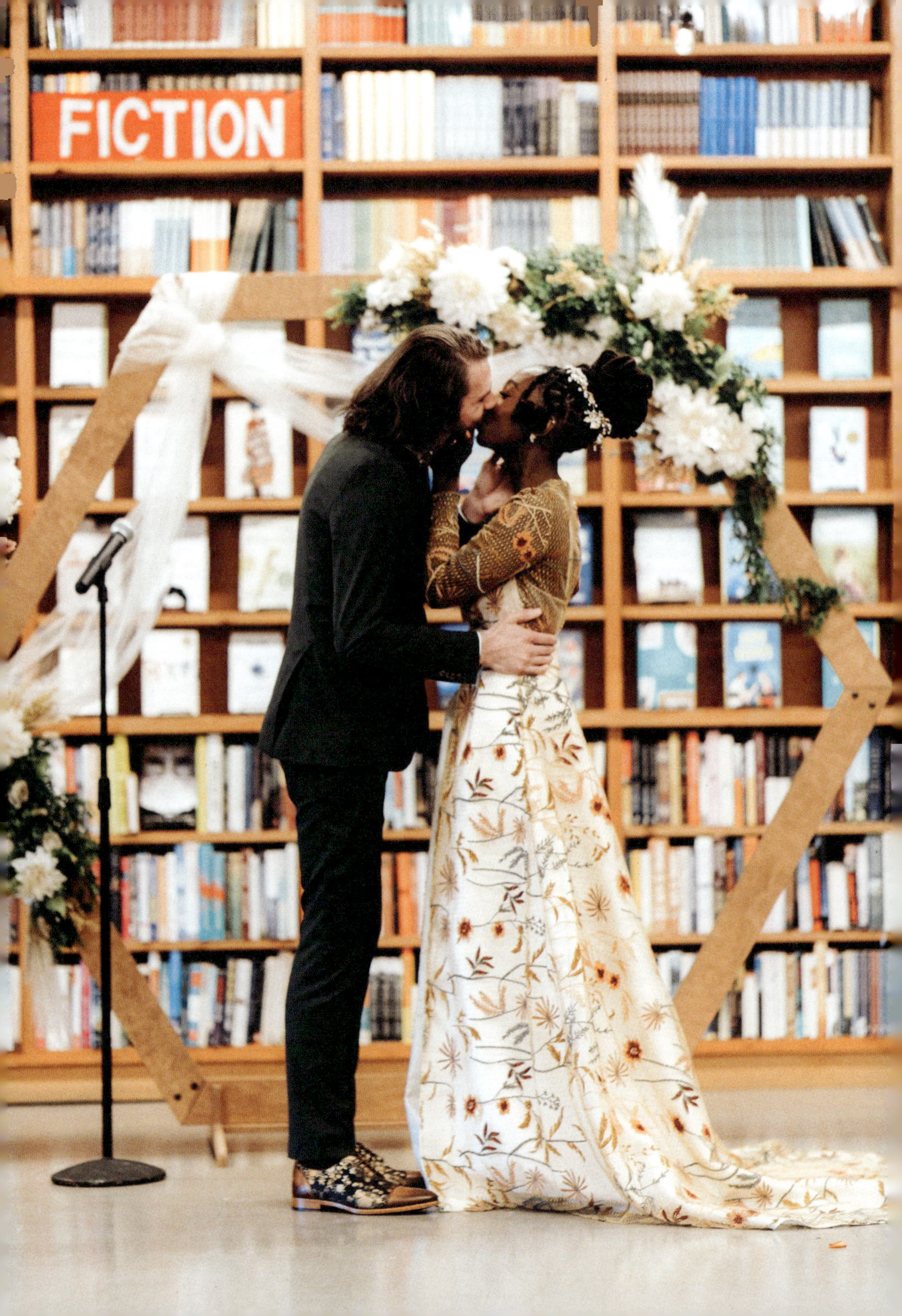
FICTION

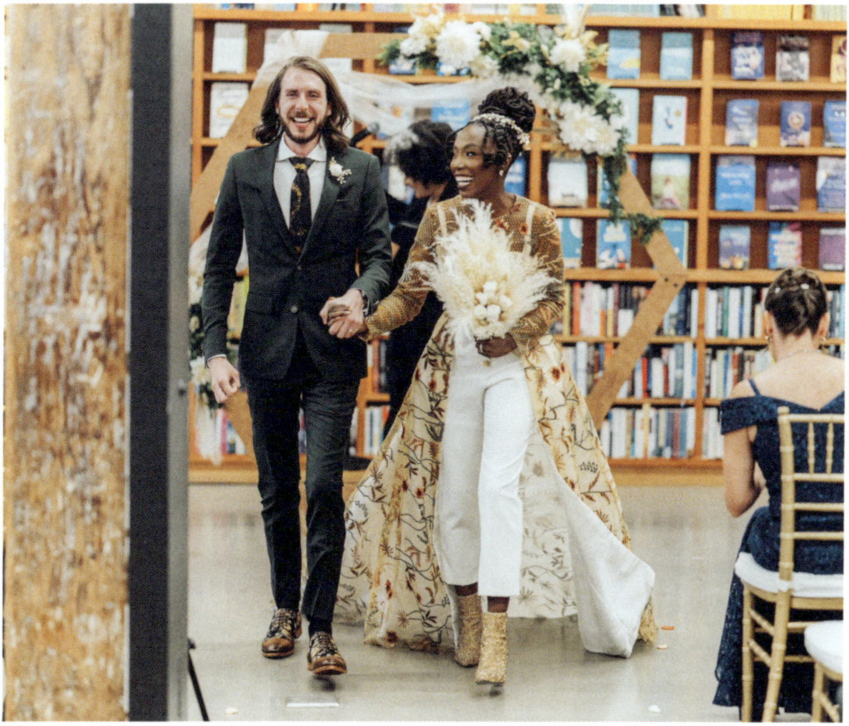

KAYLAH AND NICK

Wedding: August 8, 2022 | More Than Words (Boston, Massachusetts)

TELLING STORIES: Nick and Kaylah bonded over theater. "We both really love stories in whatever form they come. Our ideal date is seeing a movie or show, then going out for drinks after to talk about it. We love how some stories can be small and specific, yet universal in their reach."

For Kaylah and Nick, stories introduce people to new ideas and new realities. So getting married in a bookstore filled with stories turned out to be the ideal venue. "Being married in a place where we were surrounded by books, and the wonderful journeys within, felt like a perfect metaphor for the journey we were about to embark on together."

The couple didn't initially plan to say their "I do's" or hold their reception at a warehouse bookstore. But when Kaylah learned about the

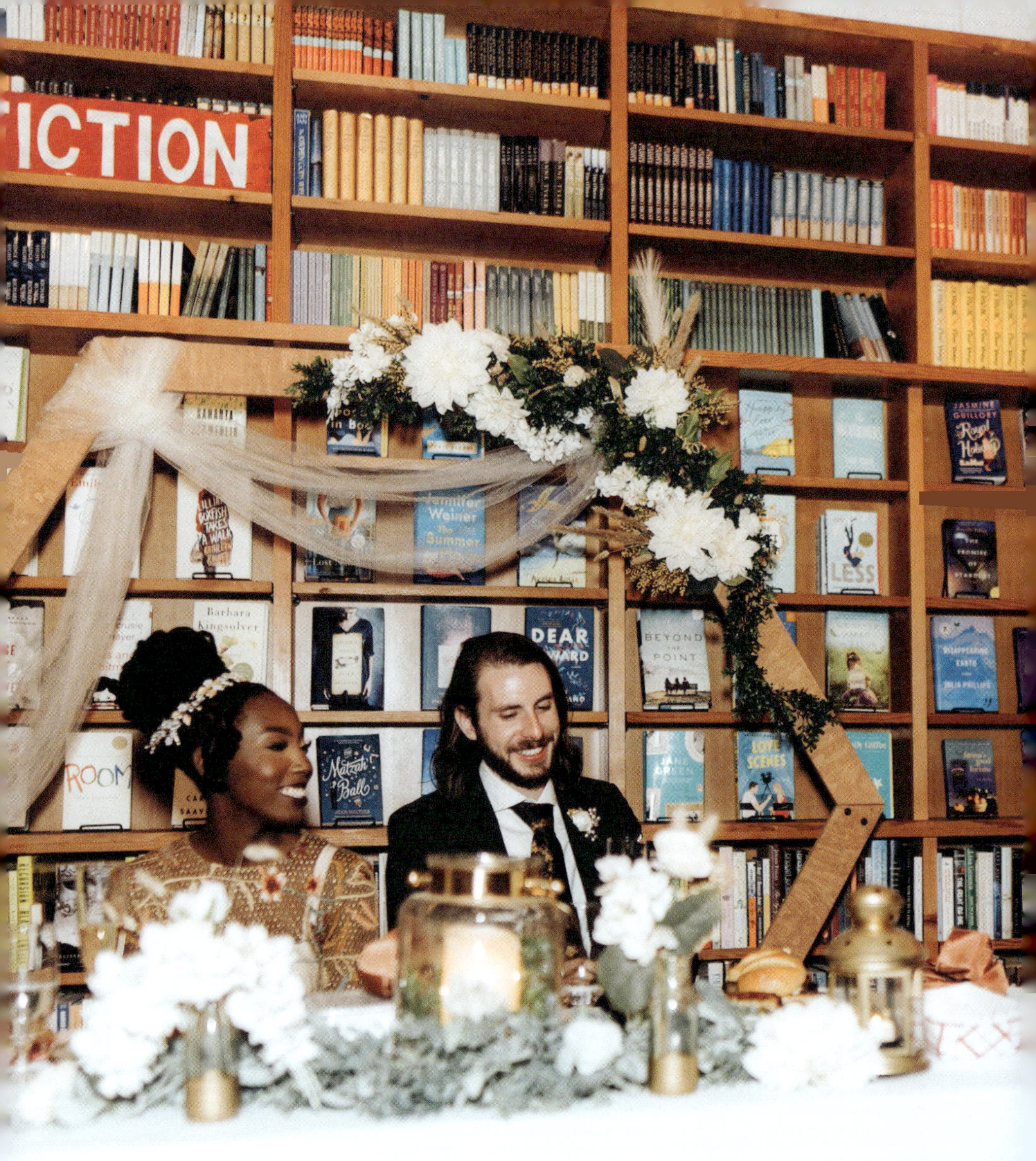
ICTION
Barbara Kingsolver
Jennifer Weiner The Summer
DEAR EDWARD
BEYOND THE POINT
LESS
ROOM
LOVE SCENES
JANE GREEN
JASMINE GUILLORY
DISAPPEARING EARTH
JULIA PHILLIPS

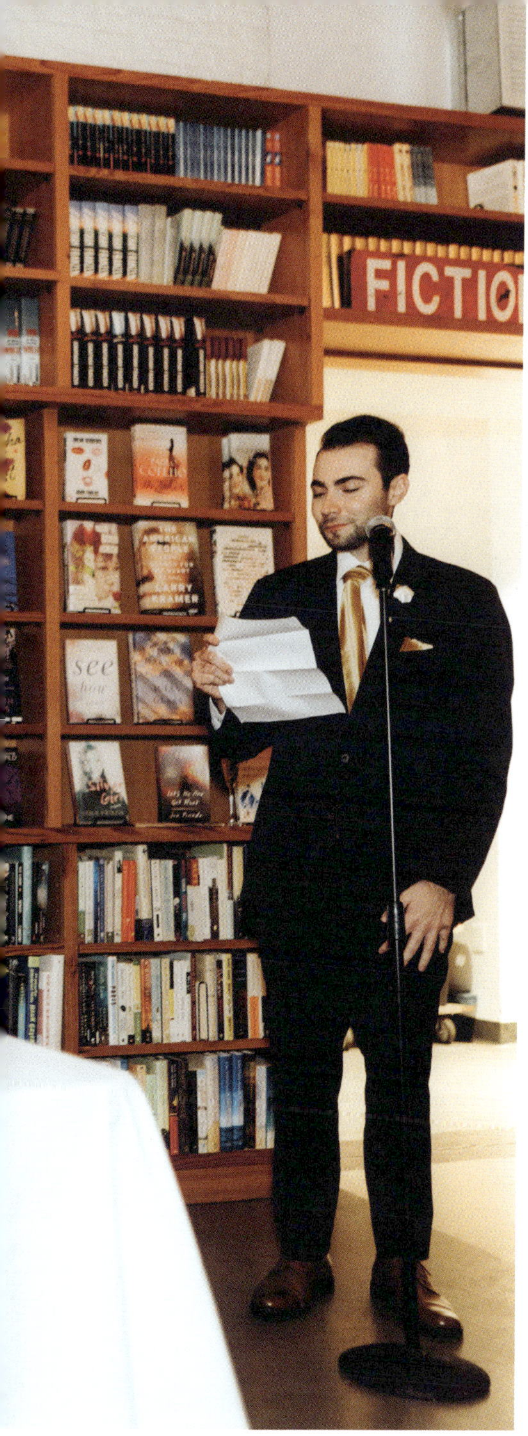

nonprofit bookstore through her work, both she and Nick were excited about getting married at More Than Words.

In addition, the store's mission to empower young people made them feel this would be "perfect." The bookstore hires young adults who are in the foster care system or are court-involved, unhoused, or not in school. The goal is to help them take charge of their lives through their work at the store.

And, of course, the importance of stories in the wedding couple's relationship made this venue ideal. As Nick said in his groom speech:

"I love that today we chose to celebrate our story surrounded by stories. They are such an integral part of why we connected in the first place. Whether we found these stories through theater, film, or TV, they continue to give us language to relate to one another, and places to escape to together."

Long live stories!

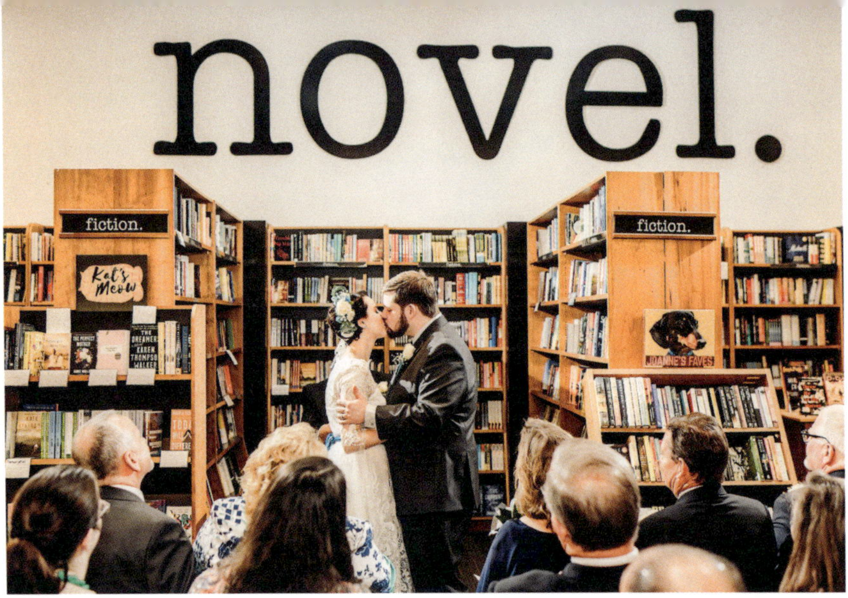

ARTHUR AND AUDREY

Wedding: June 2, 2019 | Novel Bookstore (Memphis, Tennessee)

A DATE TO REMEMBER: Audrey is one in a long line of teachers, from her mother to her great-grandmother on her mother's side. It's no surprise, then, that she was attracted to Arthur, who she started dating her senior year of college. Arthur became a teacher, too. While Audrey chose to teach history like her grandfather, Arthur prefers English.

Initially, Arthur and Audrey planned to elope. Instead, they decided on a small summer wedding with lots of photos and food. "We looked for months for an inspiring or interesting indoor location to take photos. At some point I came across an Instagram post by Novel, in which one of their employees, I think, used the building for their own small wedding," she said. Audrey reached out to see if she and Arthur could do the same.

The date the couple chose holds special significance for Audrey, whose maternal grandparents also married on June 2. Audrey wanted to give the date a new meaning not just by making it her wedding day, but also by asking her grandfather to officiate.

As if marrying in a bookstore weren't bookish enough, Arthur and Audrey brought books from their personal libraries to use as centerpieces for the dining tables. Their save-the-dates and RSVPs were modeled on library due-date cards. In lieu of a guest book, they asked each guest to sign one book on a poster of a bookcase, which they plan to frame. Maps also figured heavily at their wedding. Audrey's bouquet was made from folded-up paper maps, and maps served as the background for signage to direct their guests.

Happily their books and maps led them to the perfect wedding.

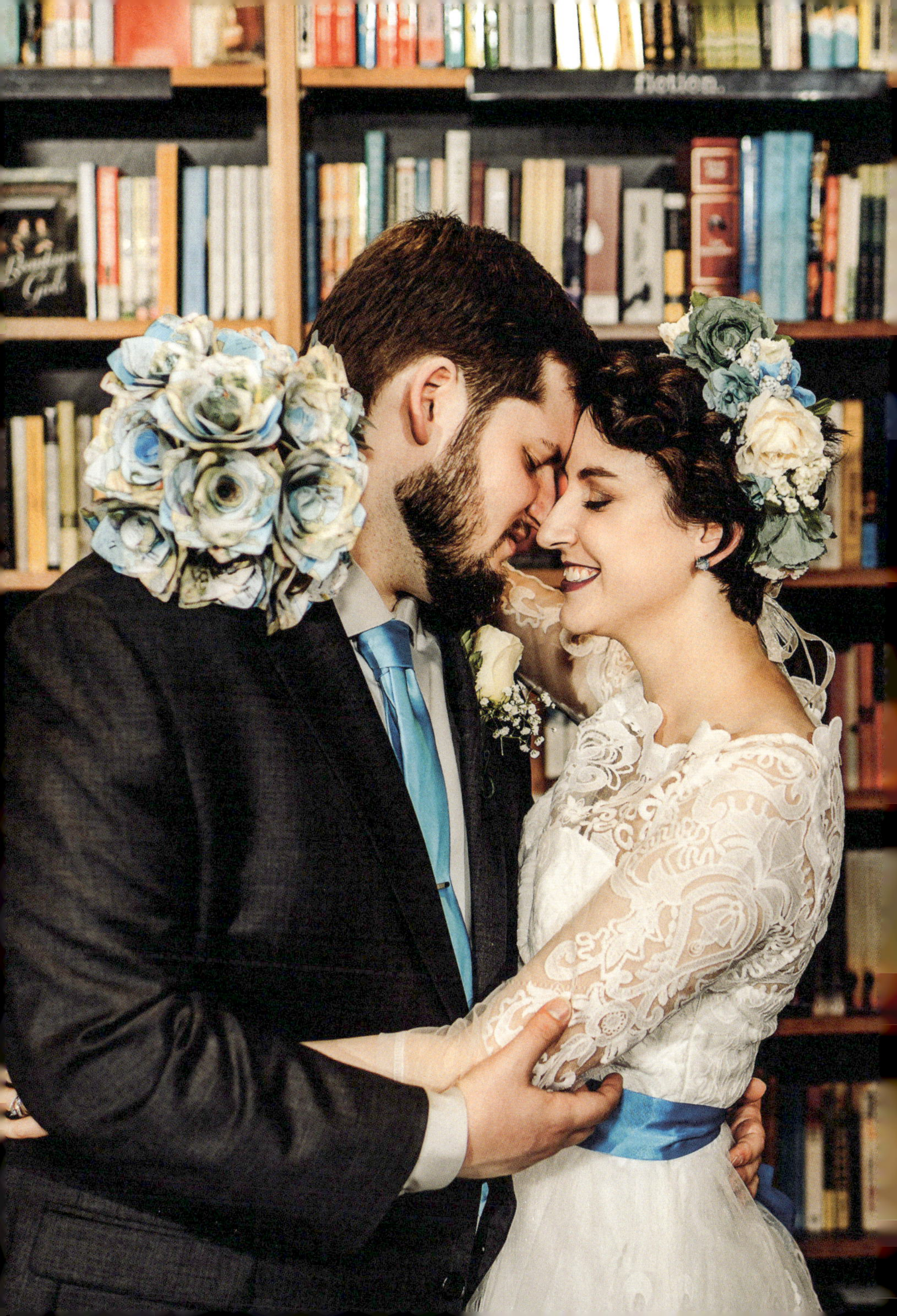
fiction.

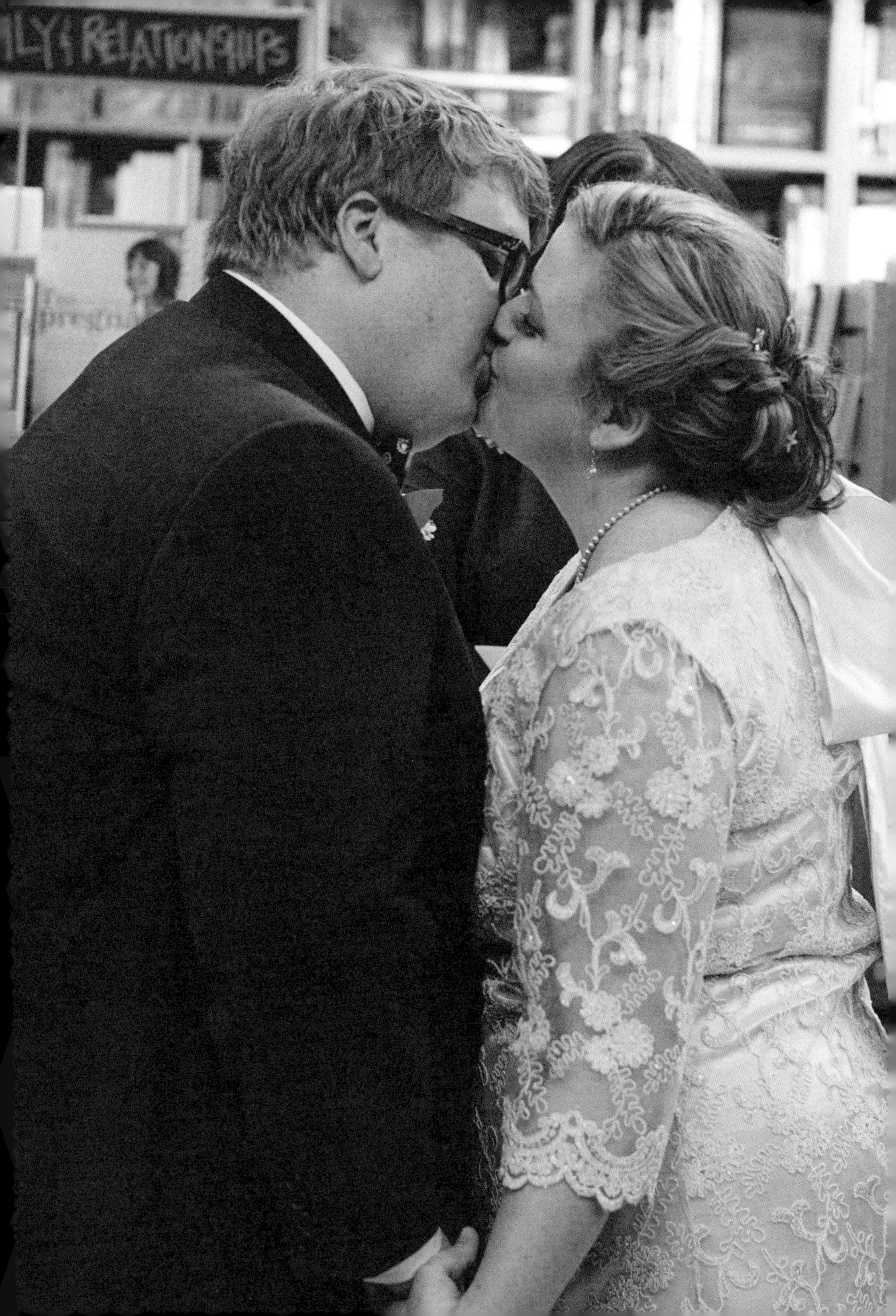
ILY & RELATIONSHIPS

ANDREW AND NIKI

Wedding: February 22, 2014 | Parnassus Books (Nashville, Tennessee)

WEDDING SURPRISE: Ann Patchett, PEN/Faulkner Award–winning author and owner of Parnassus, is no stranger to love stories, nor to weddings for that matter. So when Niki, who Patchett had known for years, and who was then events and marketing director at Parnassus—and the person who encouraged Patchett to write the essay collection *This Is the Story of a Happy Marriage*—approached her about hosting an engagement party at the store, Patchett readily agreed. But she did have one proviso: Andrew and Niki had to get married at the party. She wanted to turn it into a surprise wedding for the guests.

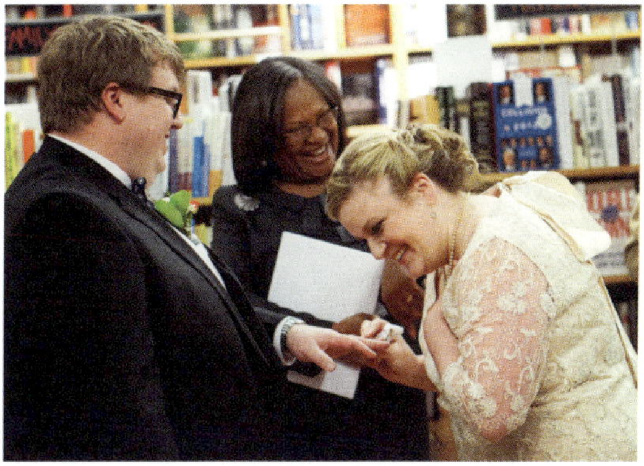

In part that's because Patchett doesn't have fond memories of the wedding industry from her work for *Bridal Guide* magazine. She thought that many weddings were "ridiculously expensive." As Patchett later wrote on the store blog, "Musing": "Niki and Andrew are fun people, and I wanted them to have a fun wedding. So the three of us decided to keep the secret."

Niki and Andrew were happy to have the pressure removed from their previously planned May wedding. A Parnassus wedding made sense, because of the role the store had played in the early days of their relationship. The pair had met the same day in 2012 that a photographer came to the store to take photos of Patchett for the *Time 100*. Later, Niki and Andrew figured out that they had met even earlier, on another significant bookstore date: the day Parnassus opened in November 2011.

The county clerk, who married the couple, was one of only a handful of people who knew their plans. Andrew and Niki didn't even tell their parents that the party was going to serve a dual purpose.

Partway through the party, Patchett made a toast. Then Andrew made a second toast, while Niki changed into her wedding dress. Five minutes later the couple were husband and wife.

"Parnassus was an amazing place to work and an amazing place to get married," Niki said, adding that she has "no regrets, none," about her surprise wedding to Andrew. "We still had a big party. It was maybe the coolest thing I'll ever do."

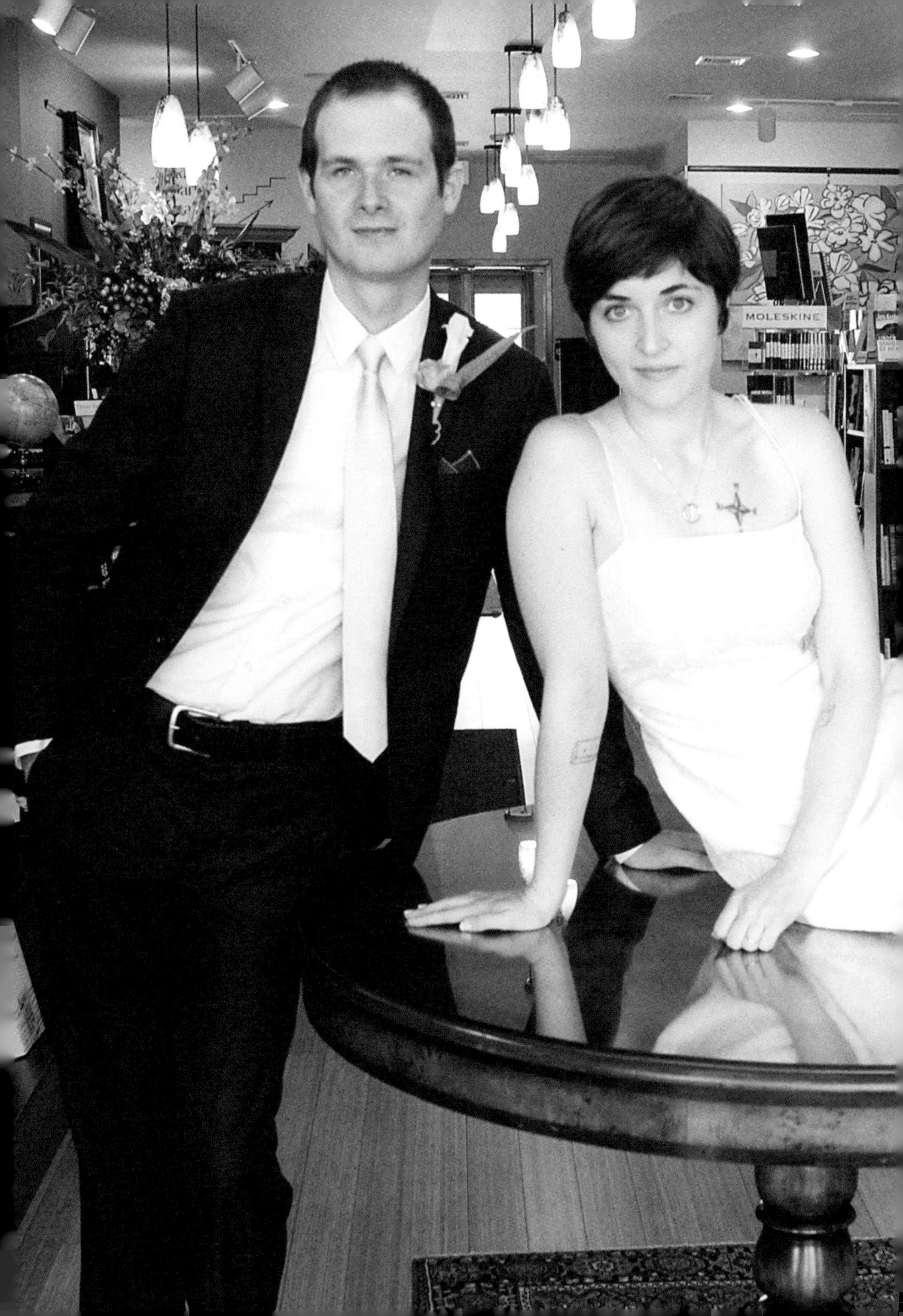
MOLESKINE

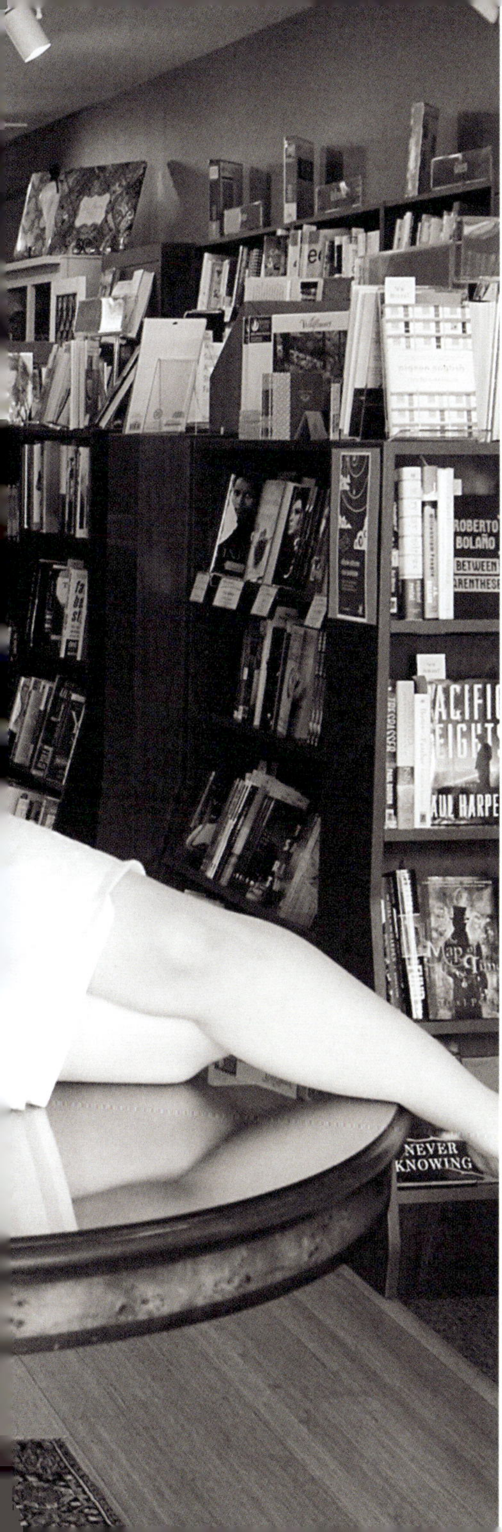

KATE AND MICHAEL

Married: July 10, 2011 | Penguin Bookshop (Sewickley, Pennsylvania)

STARTING A NEW STORY: When they fell in love and got engaged, booksellers Kate and Michael both worked at the Penguin Bookshop in the Pittsburgh suburb of Sewickley. "It just made sense to get married there," Kate said.

For her, the bookstore served as her home away from home. "I felt such community with my colleagues and the store's customers," she said. To marry there "felt much more meaningful than a hotel or an expensive venue that I had no connection to."

Plus, Kate added, "We wanted to get married surrounded by all kinds of stories, to start our own story surrounded by so many books."

They did just that. Michael and Kate exchanged vows amid friends, colleagues, and family members at a Sunday afternoon wedding, with light shining through the windows in the children's section. Afterwards, Kate's young cousins spread out and started looking at and reading books. Kate and Michael let each child select a book to take home as a memento of the special day.

A few years later Kate left bookselling, but not the book world. A fan of textiles, she published a book about working with them, which is entitled *Radical Sewing*. Kate also took a job with the Book Industry Charitable Foundation, which enabled her to stay in touch with booksellers around the country. Perhaps this new generation of booksellers will include another pair or two who, like Kate and Michael, will fall in love in a bookstore.

ABIGAIL AND JASON

Married: November 22, 2020 | Women & Children First (Chicago, Illinois)

ALL YOU NEED IS LOVE: When Covid forced Abigail and Jason to abandon their plans for a destination wedding on a beach, the couple turned to their favorite bookstore, Women & Children First, to see if they could marry there instead. Owners Sarah Hollenbeck and Lynn Mooney said yes.

Jason said that he has no regrets about their masked wedding in the science fiction section in front of an Octavia Butler display, at one of the country's few remaining feminist bookstores. "If we got married again next month, I'd want to do it the exact same way."

Plus, there was none of the stress of dealing with venues, caterers, florists, and the rest. Because they broadcast the wedding via Zoom, the couple could invite as many friends and family members as they wanted, without worrying about social distancing . . . or the cost.

While Women & Children First holds a special place in Jason and Abigail's life together, so do books in general. The couple likes to read them out loud to each other. "Reading together fosters conversations and sometimes debate, bringing our relationship to deeper levels," Jason said.

About a year after the wedding, Jason and Abigail moved away from Chicago, but they still make a point of visiting Women & Children First to restock their library and to relive at the store their early dates and wedding day. "We used to go for long walks from Rogers Park to Andersonville and would always stop in at Women & Children First, the first couple of summers we were dating," Jason said. And when their daughter was born in February 2023, they made sure that she had a Women & Children First onesie, along with plenty of books.

As for Hollenbeck and Mooney, they have no regrets either and stand by their original Facebook post: "Hosting this awesome couple's wedding at our bookstore was a much-needed bright spot in an otherwise soul-crushing year! Many congrats to Abigail & Jason! We wish you a lifetime of love and good reading."

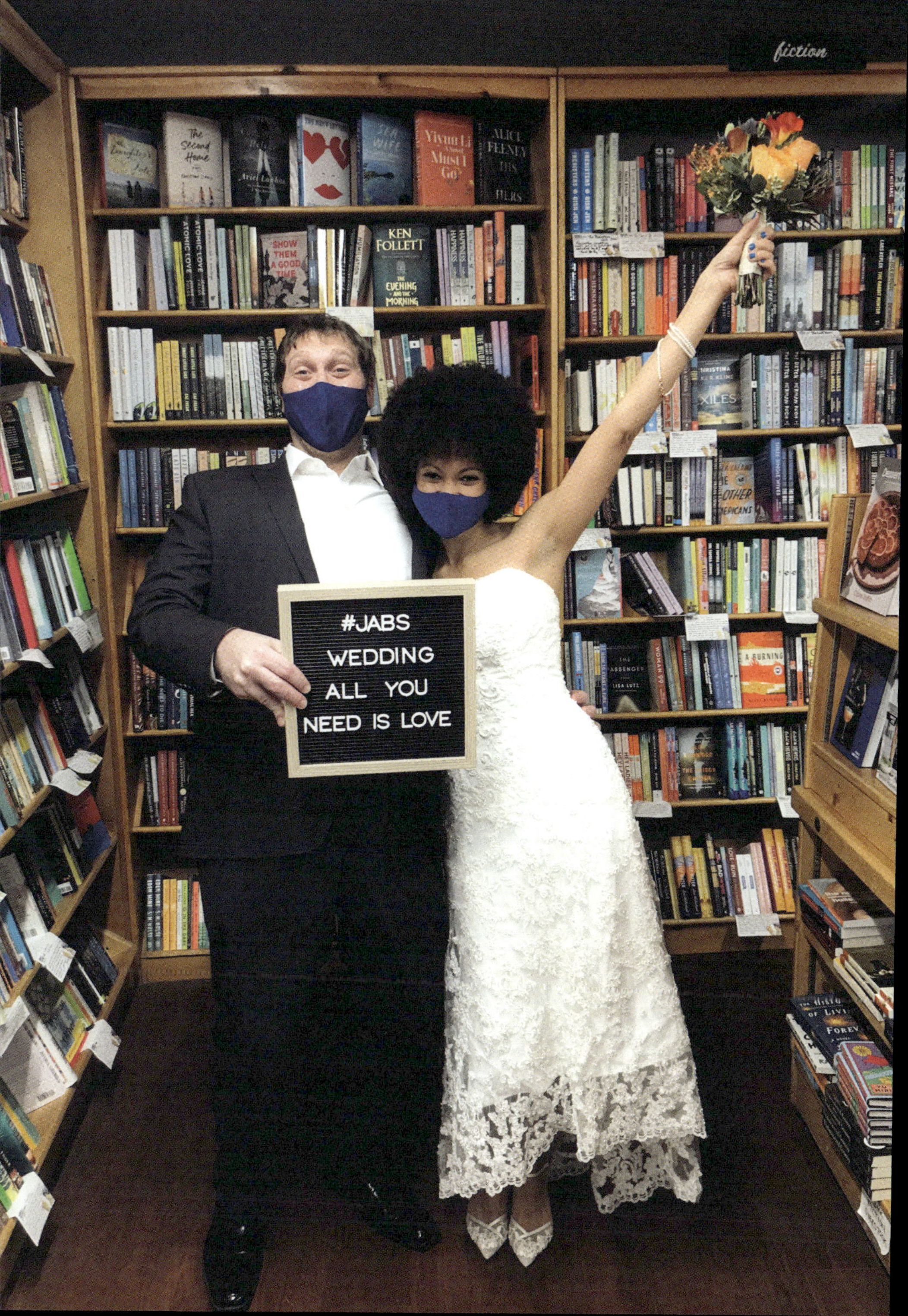
fiction
#JABS
WEDDING
ALL YOU
NEED IS LOVE

AFTERWORD

The Book Industry Charitable (Binc) Foundation is the only nonprofit in the country dedicated to assisting book and comic shop employees and owners in need.

As the safety net for booksellers and comic retailers, Binc coordinates essential programs to strengthen the book and comic-selling communities. Its core program assists employees and shop owners who have demonstrated financial need arising from severe hardship and/or emergency circumstances. Since its inception, the organization has provided over $11 million in financial assistance and scholarships to more than 10,000 families.

A portion of the proceeds from this book will be donated to further Binc's work.

ACKNOWLEDGMENTS

Many hands are credited with making light work. But in this case, they also contributed to making a better book. Thank you to Sue Berger Ramin for the concept behind this book and for believing in my ability to translate it. Thanks also to the staff at Brandeis University Press, especially Ashley Burns, who shared Sue's enthusiasm for the project. Many thanks are also owed to Lisa Diercks for her imaginative design that captures both types of love depicted in the book: for someone beloved and for bookstores. Nor would the book read as well without a big assist from Julie Allred and Zach Gillan at BW&A Books who managed production. I also would like to give a shout out to all the participating couples and one bride, who so generously shared their stories with me. May you all have found your happily ever after. A big thank you as well to the many talented photographers, whose work is showcased in the book. Every one of you made it seem easy to capture life's happiest moments. But as someone who has tried and frequently failed at making memories with my pictures, I know just how hard it is to do that well. Several photographers generously updated images for this book. Thank you. And I would be remiss not to thank my husband, Chuck, for supporting me during the many hours I spent seeking out examples of bookstore love.

ABOUT THE AUTHOR

Judith Rosen worked in publishing and bookselling for a dozen years before writing about them both as the long-time Bookselling Editor and New England Correspondent for *Publishers Weekly*. Some of her interviews and articles have been collected in *Writing for Your Life* and in *The Writer's Handbook*. She lives in Cambridge, Massachusetts.